THE BOOK OF
SPIDERS

THE BOOK OF
SPIDERS

ROD PRESTON-MAFHAM

CHARTWELL
BOOKS, INC.

Published by Chartwell Books
A Division of Book Sales Inc.
114 Northfield Avenue
Edison, New Jersey 08837
USA

Copyright ©1991 Quarto Publishing plc

This edition printed 1998

ISBN 0-7858-0953-8

QUMASPI

This book is produced by
Quantum Books Ltd
6 Blundell Street
London N7 9BH

Printed in Singapore by
Star Standard Industries Pte Ltd

CONTENTS

INTRODUCTION

That some of you have actually started to read this book is clear testimony to the fact that you are perhaps less squeamish about the subject than many people. This squeamishness is perhaps unfair to our subjects for although a number of spiders are harmful to humans, they do not seek to be so. The majority are totally harmless, and in fact are great allies in the destruction of many more harmful insect pests. Many of the jumping spiders are quite charming little creatures as can be seen from their photographs, though this may in part be due to their large front-facing eyes, which make them look almost human.

With over 30,000 species of spiders known to exist today, there are clearly limitations on the number that can be discussed in a book of 144 pages. What has been done, therefore, is to arrange the book in a number of sections that deal with the biology, life history and behavior of these animals, introducing particular species where relevant. As often as possible, these will be species with which you are likely to be familiar, either from observation in the field, or from the many superb natural-history programs on television.

The photographs are all of creatures depicted in their natural habitats, for it is only under these conditions that we can obtain a true picture of how they fit into their surroundings. The text has been made as up-to-date as possible and incorporates research into the most recent scientific literature on the subject.

SCIENTIFIC NAMES

Spiders generally lack common names, and you need to familiarize yourself with some of the relevant scientific nomenclature. The following will be of some assistance.

Each species of living organism has been given a specific biological name so that it is identifiable all around the world. These names are given in Latin so that they are recognizable in any language.

These biological names appear in italics in the text. The first word of the pair is the genus (plural genera) and always starts with a capital letter. The second word is the species name and starts with a small letter; this name, though often in Latin, may actually be descriptive of some aspect of the organism.

Each individual species referred to in the text belongs to a particular family. For example, the jumping spiders, which are mentioned quite a

This little jumping spider of the family Salticidae, *which lives in tropical rainforest in Costa Rica, shows just how attractive spiders can be. Despite the fact that it is so tiny, it does not seem to be deterred by the presence of a human. It is tilting its cephalothorax back and looking up at the photographer with its large eyes, just in case there is a meal to be had.*

lot because of their interesting lifestyles, belong to the family *Salticidae* (all family names begin with a capital letter and end in *–idae*); though terms like salticid will also be used to refer to families of spiders. Each family belongs to a suborder; the spiders belong in the suborder *Araneae*. This family in turn belongs to a yet higher level of classification, the class *Arachnida*, which in turn belongs within the phylum *Chelicerata* along with, for example, the class *Merostomata*, the king crabs.

Where possible, the common names will be used, but always at least once in the company of the specific name and also with the country of origin, for different countries may use different common names for the same species, or alternatively the same common name may be used in different countries to describe different species.

Some of the anatomical structures found within these groups again do not have common names, so you are referred to the glossary at the end of the book where many of these unfamiliar terms will be defined.

THE MEANING OF SOME SPIDER SPECIES NAMES

The meaning of some names is fairly obvious, for example, *elongate* indicates an elongate spider, *ovate* an oval spider and *triangulosa* a triangular spider. Less obvious perhaps are epithets such as *melanurum* indicating the color black and *rufipes* meaning "with red feet." Some names give an idea of where the animal lives, so that the epithet *sylvatica* means "from the woods," *domestica* means "associated with human habitation," and *maritime* perhaps more obviously means "from near the sea." Other names indicate size, *gross* indicating the animal is fairly big and *pygmaea* clearly meaning that it is small. Countries may also appear in epithets, for example the spider *Xysticus labradorensis* has an obvious origin, though *Herpyllus blackwalli* was not originally found in Blackwall, London, but is in fact named after the famous 19th-century arachnologist, John Blackwall.

Araneus quadratus (top) is named for the four white spots on the abdomen which are arranged in a rough square. Herennia ornatissima (right) from Malaysia is literally "the most ornate herennia."

CLASSIFICATION OF SPIDERS AND SCORPIONS IN THE CLASS *ARACHNIDA*

Each species of spider or scorpion belongs in a family, which in turn fits into a higher level of classification, and so on.

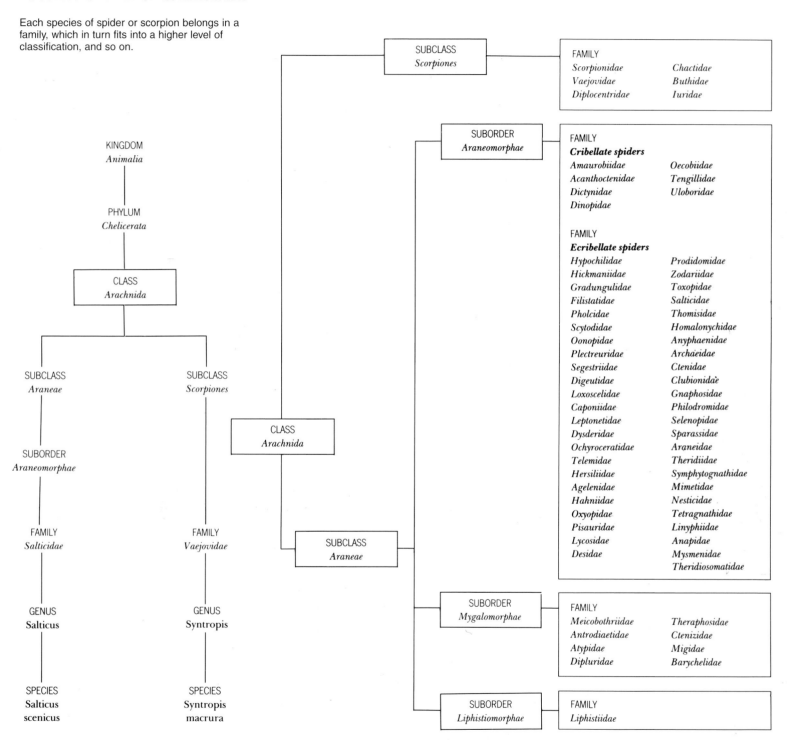

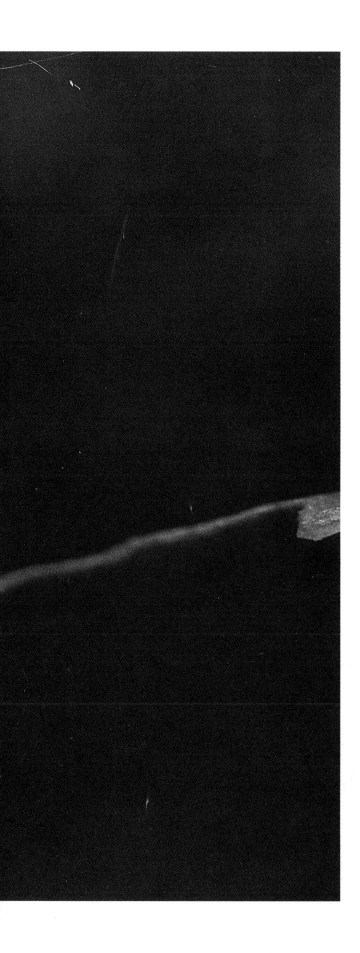

EVOLUTION AND BIOLOGY

To the uninitiated, the *Arachnida* are probably thought of as similar to insects, but with four pairs of legs, and with a similar biology. This is, however, not strictly true. Because of their carnivorous lifestyle and, at least in the spiders, their ability to produce silk, they show a number of deviations from typical arthropods.

Since all arachnids are carnivorous, they show well-developed adaptations for capturing and killing their prey; well-developed jaws, and in the spiders and scorpions a means of immobilizing the prey with poison.

Silk is produced by other insects as well, but it is only in the spiders that a variety of different types is found, each with its own special function and produced from different kinds of gland.

This bizarre Gasteracantha *spider lives in the gloomy rainforests of New Guinea. No one has yet worked out why they have such an odd shape, but it may be because this makes it difficult for a bird to hold and swallow them.*

THE ORIGINS OF THE *ARACHNIDA*

There is still some doubt as to the precise origins of the *Chelicerata*, the phylum to which the *Arachnida* belong in company with the *Merostomata* (king crabs), the *Pycnogonida* (sea spiders) and the *Eurypterida* (extinct sea scorpions). They certainly originated in the sea, and it is believed that their common ancestor was not unlike a king crab in appearance. The most recent research indicates that the orders that make up the *Arachnida* had a common ancestor, from which two distinct groups have evolved. These two groups are based on the presence or absence of extensor muscles (the muscles which straighten) within the leg. In the subclasses *Araneae* (spiders), *Amblypygi* (tailless whip scorpions), *Uropygi* (tailed whip scorpions) and *Acari* (mites and ticks), the extensor muscles are primitively absent. In the *Scorpiones* (scorpions), *Pseudoscorpiones* (false or pseudoscorpions) and *Solifugae* (sun spiders), extensor muscles are present.

Included with this latter group is the order *Opiolines* (harvestmen) which, although they lack extensor muscles, have too much in common with the other three orders not to be included with them.

Like the other arthropod groups, the arachnids have a tough external skeleton, the exoskeleton, which is made up of a series of plates and cylinders within which lie the muscle systems and other soft organs. The arachnids differ from the other arthropod groups, however, through having four pairs of walking legs; for the *Hexapoda*, which includes the insects, have three pairs, the crustaceans five pairs and the myriapods (centipedes and millipedes) have many pairs. Apart from the difference in the number of pairs of legs, the arachnids diverge from the insects in the way in which the body is divided up. In the insects, the body is divided into head, thorax and abdomen, whereas in the arachnids the head and thorax are fused together in some groups to form the prosoma (or cephalothorax), and in others all three divisions are fused into a single structure. Another distinction is that insects always have a pair of antennae.

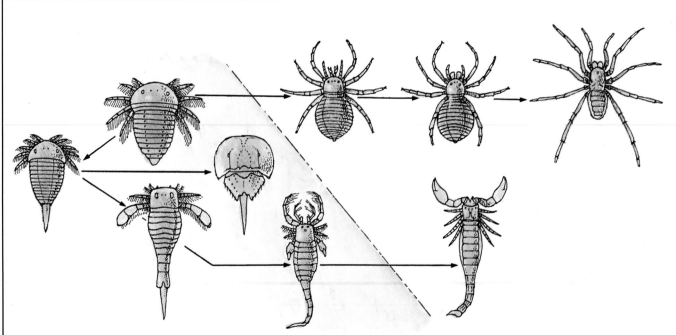

ARACHNID ORIGINS

We can only guess at what the ancestors of spiders and scorpions might have looked like, since their fossil record is very limited. This diagram shows what they may have looked like, and how they relate to the fossils that have been found and to present living groups. The hypothetical chelicerate arachnid ancestor probably existed at least 250 million years before the first spider. From this aquatic creature, two separate lines developed, one of which gave rise to the spiders, possibly via the extinct *Trigonotarbi*. It also gave rise to the common ancestor of the *Merostomata* (king crabs) and the aquatic *Eurypterida*, from which the scorpions evolved.

FOSSIL RECORD

The fossil record of the spiders (*Araneae*) is not very good, for they are relatively soft-bodied creatures and therefore do not easily fossilize. It is from around the Middle Devonian rocks, some 380–385 million years old, that the earliest indications of spiders have been found. The evidence consists of a recently discovered, nearly complete spider spinneret whose structure is quite advanced, an indication that spiders may already have been in existence for a considerable time, though the spinneret's relationship to those of contemporary spider families is not yet clear. No fossils of flying insects have been found from as early as this, and it may therefore be assumed that it was a predator of ground-dwelling arthropods.

THE ARACHNIDS AND THEIR ALLIES

Spiders and scorpions are arthropods belonging to the class *Arachnida*. They are clearly distinguishable from the other arthropods, most easily by counting the number of pairs of legs. Insects possess three pairs; spiders and scorpions possess four pairs; crustaceans have five pairs; and centipedes and their cousins the millipedes have many pairs. Spiders and scorpions also lack the antennae characteristic of

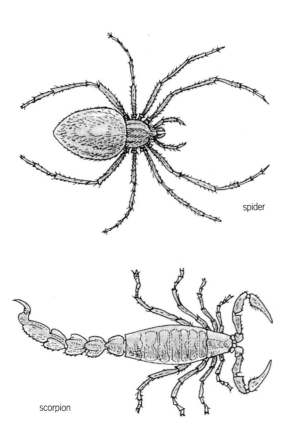

spider

scorpion

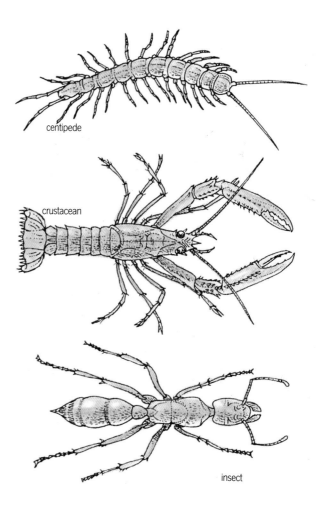

centipede

crustacean

insect

LIVING SPIDERS

The families of living spiders have representatives in all regions of the world; in fact anywhere that segmented insects, or arthropods, are found, spiders are likely to be preying on them. There are even some spiders that live on the seashore, where they are submerged beneath the ocean twice a day. In fresh water there is, of course, the well-known water spider, *Argyroneta aquatica*, which is habitually aquatic, though other species are able to submerge themselves when threatened or else hunt on the water surface. Many spiders are restricted to cave systems, and really the only places lacking spiders are the snowy wastes at the North and South poles, the deep sea and inside active volcanoes.

In size they vary from the giant theraphosid bird-eating spiders, whose legs would span a dinnerplate, down to the symphytognathids, which could sit quite happily on, and just about span, the eye of one of the aforementioned giants. The largest spiders in terms of leg-span are male theraphosids from the jungles of South America, which may have a body up to 3 in (75 mm) in length with a span across the legs of some 10 in (255 mm). Females tend to have larger bodies, up to 3.5 in (90 mm) in length, but with a smaller leg-span of only 9 in (230 mm). These giant females may weigh as much as 3 oz (80 g).

At the other extreme are spiders belonging to the families *Anapidae*, *Symphytognathidae* and *Mysmenidae*, which live among debris on the soil surface, many of whom are smaller than a pinhead. The restriction of these tiny spiders to damp moss or leaf litter is an adaptation to reduce the risk of death from dehydration; to farther reduce water loss, some of these spiders are covered in thick, armored plate. Despite their minuscule size, some of them are known to spin tiny orb webs.

MYGALOMORPHS AND ARANEOMORPHS

The spiders are divided into three suborders, the primitive *Liphistiomorphae*, which retain the same segmentation of the abdomen as their ancestors, the *Mygalomorphae* and the *Araneomorphae*. There is little more to be said about the liphistiomorphs except that they come from tropical Asia and, being burrowing spiders, are seldom seen. All of the spiders included in this book belong to the following two groups:

1 The *Mygalomorphae*, now referred to by many people as "tarantulas," but wrongly so, for the true tarantulas are araneomorph spiders of the widespread genus *Lycosa*.

2 The *Araneomorphae*, usually called the "true spiders."

Of the two, the mygalomorphs are the more primitive and to many people the more repulsive, since they contain the large, hairy, bird-eating spiders so beloved of movie-makers. There is, however, a proportion of the world's population that actually enjoys the company of this family, for a number of them are now popular as household pets. This has unfortunately endangered a few species, but now that some can be bred in captivity, removal of adults from the wild may at last cease.

Apart from the fact that the mygalomorph spiders are, on the whole, larger than the araneomorphs, the most obvious and visible difference between them is the way in which the jaws work. The jaws of mygalomorphs strike downward, whereas the jaws of araneomorphs oppose each other (see the diagrams below).

Many of the mygalomorphs construct burrows both to hide from their enemies and to escape the rigors of the environments in which they live, for most species inhabit the warmer parts of the world.

The vast bulk of spiders are araneomorphs and the group includes about 50 families. Some of these families are small, obscure, or unlikely to be seen by the average reader, and unless there is something special or interesting about them, they are not mentioned here. Of the 50 or so families from around the world, only seven are cribellate, with the majority being ecribellate (see page 21).

A life-size drawing of one of the world's largest spiders, belonging to the genus Theraphosa. *Because they often hunt on trees and may take sitting female birds from the nest, they are commonly called bird-eating spiders. In contrast, the world's smallest spiders are no bigger than a pinhead.*

ARACHNID RELATIONSHIPS

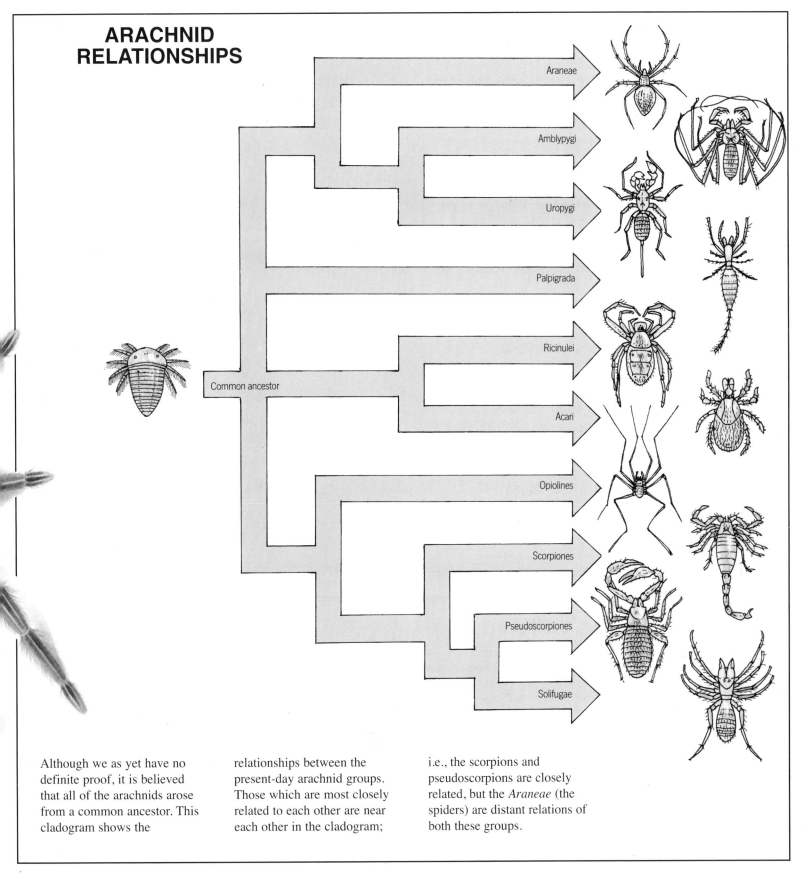

Common ancestor

Araneae

Amblypygi

Uropygi

Palpigrada

Ricinulei

Acari

Opiolines

Scorpiones

Pseudoscorpiones

Solifugae

Although we as yet have no definite proof, it is believed that all of the arachnids arose from a common ancestor. This cladogram shows the relationships between the present-day arachnid groups. Those which are most closely related to each other are near each other in the cladogram; i.e., the scorpions and pseudoscorpions are closely related, but the *Araneae* (the spiders) are distant relations of both these groups.

DEADLY SCORPIONS

The group which probably strikes almost as much fear into people as snakes, and perhaps more than spiders, and rightly so, are the scorpions. One obvious reason is that in the countries where scorpions are found, the more venomous species may account annually for a considerable number of deaths, especially in very young children. Scorpions are mainly tropical and subtropical in distribution with representatives in all continents, though in Europe they are, with the exception of one species, restricted to the Mediterranean region. The British Isles has no naturally occurring species, though a colony of the harmless southern European *Euscorpius flavicaudis* has existed, possibly for as long as 100 years, in walls in the old dockyard in Sheerness, Kent. More than 50 species occur in the warmer parts of the U.S.A., and some of them are very poisonous.

The different species of scorpions show a considerable range of body sizes. The smallest known species, *Typhlochactas mitchelli*, is a blind leaf-litter-dwelling scorpion from southern Mexico, which attains a length of around 0.4 in (9 mm), while the largest species, *Pandinus giganticus* from tropical Africa, may reach nearly 8 in (200 mm) in length. In color they tend to be shades of light to dark brown and black, though the large forest scorpions of tropical Asia, which may attain lengths of as much as 5 in (130 mm), are a brilliant dark bottle-green.

The closeup of the face of a giant crab spider (above left), which lives cryptically on tree trunks in the Malaysian forest, clearly shows the sideways-striking jaws typical of araneomorph spiders. The South African baboon spider Harpactira *(above right), on the other hand, is a mygalomorph and its large, downward-striking jaws can be seen projecting forward in front of its head.* Araniella cucurbitina *(right) is found in both Europe and the U.S.A., where its orb web may often be seen in suburban yards. This particular specimen has captured an unpalatable burnet moth much bigger than itself, a demonstration of the efficiency of the araneomorph jaw action.*

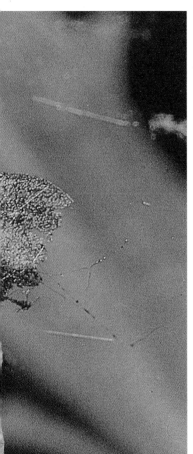

JAW MECHANISMS

The primitive *Liphistiidae* and the mygalomorph spiders have their jaws arranged so that they strike down against prey walking on the ground or some other hard surface. Araneomorph spiders' jaws work independent from any surface, since they move toward each other when in action. The prey becomes impaled between them. The latter system is much more efficient, since it allows a spider to catch prey on the flimsy structure to its web, an action which would certainly be precluded in the mygalomorph system.

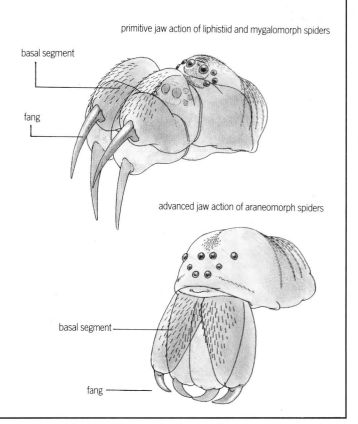

primitive jaw action of liphistiid and mygalomorph spiders

basal segment

fang

advanced jaw action of araneomorph spiders

basal segment

fang

ODD SHAPES IN SPIDERS

Although the majority of species fit the basic outline that most of us would recognize as being that of a typical spider, there are a number of families with members who have evolved bizarre body shapes. In some instances, we are able to understand why these particular shapes have evolved, while in others we are still guessing. Some shapes we know are related to mimicry of inanimate objects which helps the spider to hide from its enemies; other shapes may make it difficult for a predator to get hold of the spider if it finds it, while yet other adaptations in the basic spider shape are associated with sex differences and the mating process. Whatever these odd shapes are for, they have produced some very bizarre and interesting creatures for us to study and wonder at.

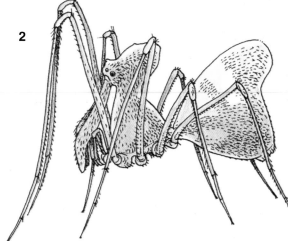

UNUSUAL CARAPACES

In a number of species in the large family *Linyphiidae*, the males have developed some very peculiar carapace modifications. It would appear that during mating the female grasps these knobs or other protuberances in her jaws, thereby preventing her from attacking and eating her mate. Below is a spider with a fairly typical carapace with which to compare the others.

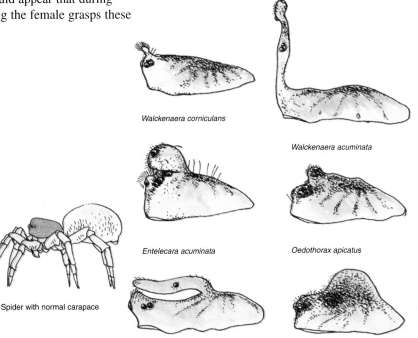

Walckenaera corniculans

Walckenaera acuminata

Entelecara acuminata

Oedothorax apicatus

Spider with normal carapace

Walckenaera furcillata

Oedothorax gibbosus

1 and *2* These two spiders are members of the very ancient family Archaeidae, *which was first described from a fossil in Baltic amber before living members were found in Madagascar, Australia, South Africa, New Zealand, and a possible finding in South America. The extremely elevated head and very long jaws may help these tiny spiders catch their prey, which consists of other species of spiders.*

3, 4 and *5* Some tropical and subtropical members of the orb-web-building family Araneidae, such as the Micrathena *left and the two different species of* Gasteracantha *below, have evolved a series of odd body shapes. It is believed that the projections and the wide body may make it difficult for birds to grasp hold of them, though no one is absolutely sure.*

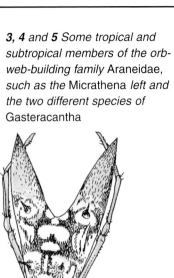

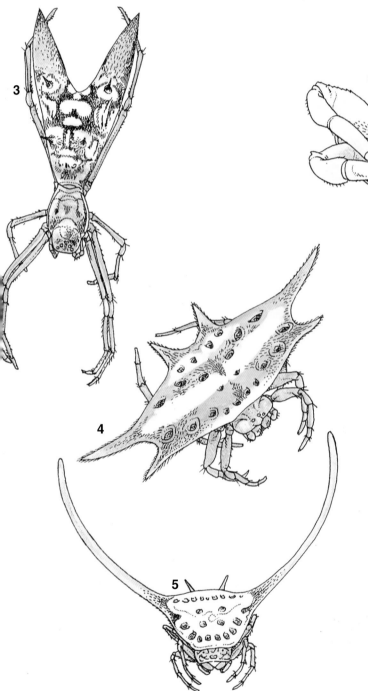

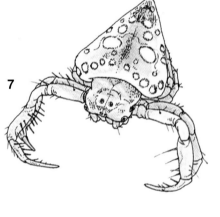

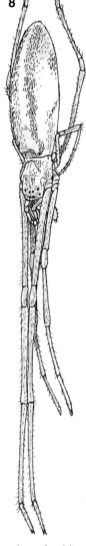

6 There is no real explanation for the odd shape and coloration of this Arcys *from Australia.*

7 Epicadus heterogaster *from the rainforest of Brazil is one of the so-called flower spiders. It may be found sitting on white flowers where it is well camouflaged, or on leaves where it resembles a complex white flower itself.*

8 A number of spiders, such as this Tetragnatha extensa, *have evolved long bodies so that they can lie cryptically along stems and leaves, hidden from their predators and in wait for possible prey items.*

EVOLUTION AND BIOLOGY

STRUCTURE OF SPIDERS

The spider body is subdivided into two parts. The cephalothorax (prosoma) is made up of the fused head and thorax, and it is joined to the abdomen (opisthosoma) by means of a narrow waist, the pedicel. The upper surface of the cephalothorax bears a hardened shield somewhat akin to that of crabs and bearing the same name, the carapace. The front end of the carapace representing the head is usually somewhat elevated and bears

the eyes, normally eight in number, but sometimes six, four, or two. In at least one species, only a single, central eye is present, formed by the fusion of a pair of eyes, while in many cave-dwelling species the eyes are vestigial or absent.

THE ABDOMEN

Except in the primitive spiders of the family *Liphistiidae*, the abdomen shows no external signs of segmentation. Its first segment is represented by the slim waist, which connects it to the cephalothorax.

Although in many spiders the abdomen is roughly globular or shortly

EXTERNAL FEATURES

Although the diagrams represent an araneomorph spider, the basic structure outlined is also true for the liphistiomorphs and the mygalomorphs. The separation of the head region and the thorax region of the

cephalothorax is not always as clearly marked as it is here. And the epigyne is very much simpler in the more primitive spiders, appearing simply as a small, slitlike opening on the underside with no accompanying ornamentation. The markings on the cephalothorax and abdomen in some instances

indicate the positions of attachment of the body muscles inside the exoskeleton. The position and number of eyes on the head varies from family to family and is used in distinguishing one from another.

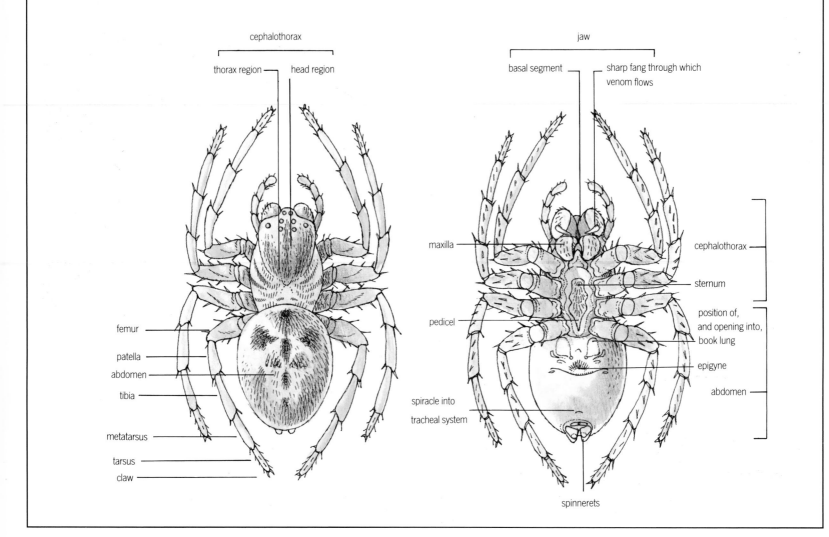

tubular, it can assume some bizarre shapes, and in some instances may bear spines or other outgrowths. Externally, there is little to see on the upper surface, but beneath may be found the openings to the book lungs and tracheae, through which the animal breathes, and also the centrally placed genital opening. This is present in the female spider with its associated epigyne. At the rear of the abdomen is the anal tubercle through which the spider voids its waste, and around or fairly close to this is the cluster of fingerlike spinnerets through which the animal secretes its silk. In primitive spiders there were eight spinnerets, which still exist, though sometimes in a nonfunctional form, in the majority of true spiders today.

In certain families of spiders, the anterior median pair of spinnerets have become modified to form a special structure, the cribellum, which produces a special, multistranded silk that is combed out by a row of special hairs, the calamistrum, on the metatarsus of the fourth pair of legs. Spiders which have a cribellum are referred to as cribellate, whereas those which lack one are referred to as ecribellate. The typical ecribellate spider retains three pairs of spinnerets in a close-knit group, with the anterior median pair reduced structurally in various ways so as to be nonfunctional. In the mygalomorph spiders, where the use of silk has become of decreased importance, there may be only two pairs of spinnerets remaining.

THE CEPHALOTHORAX

Within the cephalothorax lie the venom glands, though in a few instances these are restricted to the inside of the basal segment of the jaws. In one family, the *Scytodidae* or spitting spiders, the venom glands are greatly enlarged to produce, as well as some venom, a large amount of sticky gum. Also here is the front end of the nervous system, which is enlarged to form the spider's brain; from this the main nerve cord runs through the waist and into the abdomen. Behind the brain is a specialized stomach

The female Gea *(left) from Malaysia, demonstrates well the outline of a typical spider. On the other hand* Gasteracantha falcicornis *from southern Africa (above) gives us an idea of how evolution can affect the typical spider in attaining some special goal. It has a broad, flattened body with spiny projections, which it is believed make it difficult for birds to grasp.*

with which the spider sucks up the liquid formed by the external digestion of its prey (see page 23).

INTERNAL ORGANS

The abdomen contains the major part of the spider's internal organs – heart, main artery, and alimentary canal, which pumps blood forward through the main artery. For breathing, the abdomen may contain one or two pairs of book lungs and/or a system of tracheal tubes, branches of which may also extend through into the cephalothorax. Also present are the silk glands, the excretory (Malpighian) tubules and the reproductive organs, ovaries or testes depending upon the spider's sex.

INTERNAL STRUCTURE

Although the internal structure is basically the same in all groups, there are a number of variations that need to be considered. Only one of the seven different types of silk gland is shown; they vary from family to family. Mygalomorph spiders do not have a tracheal system, but instead have two pairs of book lungs, while some tiny spiders lack these and have only a tracheal system. The large muscles that run from the throat and stomach to the wall of the cephalothorax drive the "pump" by which spiders suck up their liquid food. This is a female spider; in a male, the ovary would be replaced by testes and the spermatheca would not be present.

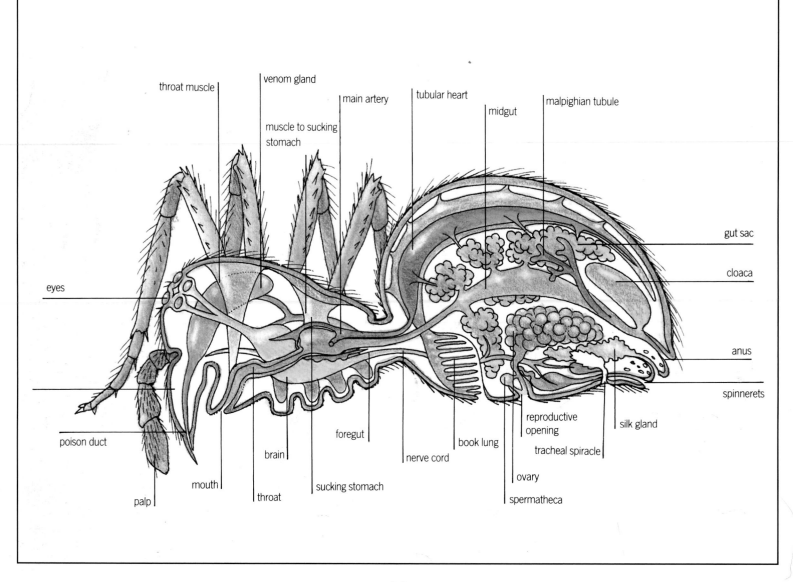

FEEDING

Like all animals, spiders need food in order to grow and eventually produce eggs and sperm to give rise to the next generation. Spiders can, in fact, live for quite a long time, often months, without food as long as they have a regular supply of water. They feed mainly upon other arthropods, although some of the larger mygalomorph spiders will take small birds and other vertebrates. Small bats have been found in the orb webs of certain of the large, rainforest-dwelling araneids.

EXTERNAL DIGESTION

In all but one spider family, which has apparently lost the ability to do so, the spider injects its prey with venom to immobilize it. It may then break up the prey with its jaws and pour powerful digestive enzymes from the maxillary glands onto it. These enzymes gradually digest the prey's internal organs, and the spider then sucks up the liquid produced by the digestive process into its alimentary canal. The action of its jaws and the processes of digestion gradually reduce the prey to a shattered mass of indigestible remains which the spider then discards. Alternatively, if the prey is an insect with a particularly tough exoskeleton, the spider pierces holes through this and pours in its digestive enzymes. Once digestion is complete and the spider has sucked out the contents, it discards the empty husk.

THE INTERNAL PROCESS

The wall of the sucking stomach is attached to the exoskeleton by means of powerful muscles which, when they contract, enlarge the stomach's capacity, drawing liquid in from the gullet (esophagus). In order to prevent the passage of any undigested particles of food into the intestine, the mouth and throat are lined with a system of hairs, which acts as a filter. Particles trapped in this filter are then washed back out of the mouth with secretions of digestive juices from the maxillary glands. The liquid food is then forced on down the intestine by the contraction of a set of circular muscles which surround the sucking stomach, their action reducing its volume. A valve prevents the liquid from being forced back into the gullet.

The liquid food now passes into the spider's midgut, where digestion continues and the products of digestion are absorbed into the body fluid, bathing the internal organs. The actual digestive and absorptive surface is increased by a series of sacs or diverticula, which branch off from the wall of the midgut. In some families they are so extensive that they penetrate into the cephalothorax. Arising from the wall of the final section of the alimentary canal, the hindgut, is a sac, the cloaca, which stores any waste food until it can be passed out of the anal pore as feces.

Nitrogenous waste produced by the body is removed by a kind of kidney, the Malpighian tubules. These secrete substances called guanates which pass into the cloaca, where they are passed out of the body along with waste from the alimentary canal.

This female Argiope *(below) from Kenya has caught a grasshopper in her orb web and has wrapped it in silk to subdue it. She now has her fangs embedded in it and is injecting it with poison to kill it before she starts to feed.*

BLOOD AND BREATHING

Spiders possess an "open circulatory system," i.e., the blood, instead of flowing through a closed system of vessels, just fills the spaces between the body wall and the internal organs. Blood is pumped through the system, but it is not as efficient as the closed system of vessels that is found in humans, for example. The heart is a longitudinal tube running along the upper surface of the abdominal cavity. Blood from this cavity, which has already passed over the abdominal organs, passes into the heart through a number of holes along its length. The heart then contracts and forces blood forward along a main artery into the cephalothorax, where it is distributed to the head and appendages. The blood then empties into the cavity of the cephalothorax and makes its way back through the waist into the abdominal cavity again, from where the cycle restarts. Valves are present where the blood enters the heart to prevent backflow into the abdominal cavity when the heart contracts and sends the blood on its way to repeat the cycle.

GAS-EXCHANGE MECHANISMS

Unlike humans, spiders do not breathe in the strict sense of the word, but they do have gas exchange-mechanisms.

The most primitive of these is the book lung, so called because its structure resembles the pages of a book. The book lung is a chamber containing a structure that resembles a pile of hollow plates, which are kept separate from each other by tiny pillars. Blood passing between these plates on its way back to the heart picks up oxygen, which diffuses from the outside into the hollow within the plate and then through the plate wall (see the diagram below).

The second mechanism for gas exchange is the tracheal system. This is a set of parallel tubes, held open by stiff muscular rings, which pass from an external spiracular opening directly to the particular body organs they are designed to serve. As oxygen is used up by these organs, a further supply diffuses along the tracheae to them.

It would appear that the tracheal system is a more efficient mechanism than the book lung, for the most primitive spiders possess two pairs of the latter, more advanced spiders have one pair of book lungs and also some tracheae, while the most advanced types have tracheae only.

BLUE-BLOODED SPIDERS

Spiders' blood does not contain red blood cells like human blood, although it does contain a blue pigment called hemocyanin. Whether this has the same role as the hemoglobin in human blood, that is, transporting oxygen around the body, is uncertain. It is probable that the spider can obtain enough oxygen for its needs from what is dissolved in the blood, and that the extra oxygen held by the hemocyanin is for use in emergencies, for example, if it has to make a sudden rapid movement to escape its enemies. There are a few cells in spiders' blood, but these are probably the equivalent of human white blood cells and are concerned with defense against infection and healing of wounds.

BOOK-LUNG STRUCTURE

The book lung operates passively. There is no pumping mechanism to force air in and out; as oxygen diffuses into the blood, so more diffuses into the system from outside. The spaces supported by pillars are kept open to the air, while the alternate spaces between them are filled with blood under pressure, which keeps them open. Oxygen in the air spaces can diffuse across the walls that separate the two and thus into the blood.

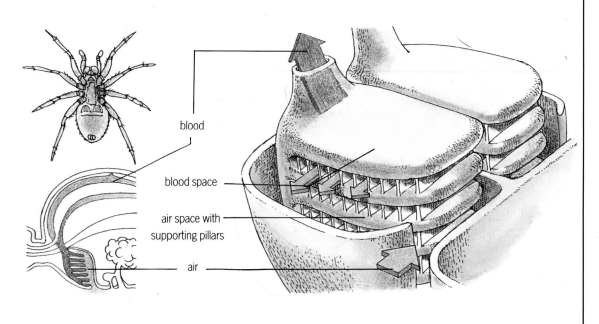

blood

blood space

air space with supporting pillars

air

REPRODUCTION

The internal structure of male and female spiders' reproductive systems is fairly straightforward. Females have two ovaries, each with an oviduct which connects to a single uterus and vagina, the latter opening to the exterior through the genital pore. The female also possesses at least one pair of sacs, called spermathecae, which are used to store sperm after mating until the eggs are ready to be fertilized. Males have a number of testes within the abdomen with tubes leading to the exterior through the genital pore.

Spider reproduction is made complex by the manner in which the sperm is introduced into the female. This process is carried out by the highly modified palpal organ on the tip of the male palp. In its simplest form, the palpal organ resembles an eye-dropper, with a flexible bulb containing a reservoir from which runs a coiled tube into which sperm can be sucked. This tube runs to the outside through a stiff spur known as the embolus, which is inserted into the female epigyne. The whole palpal organ, when not in use, lies inside the alveolus, a hollow in the last segment of the palp. The sperm can then be deposited into the female's spermathecae by squeezing the sperm out of the tube through the embolus. In the majority of spiders, however, the structure of the palp has become very complicated, and the opening to the spermathecae in the female has become associated with the epigyne (see box).

COMPLEMENTARY PARTNERS

In order for successful mating to take place, the structure of the male palp has to be complementary to that of the female epigyne, much like a key and lock mechanism. If mating is attempted between two different

Misumena vatia *females are much larger than their mates (left), but they have a very good relationship. The male is able to run around on his spouse and mate with her at will without apparently being in danger at any time. In this instance, he is even less at risk, for she is busy eating a large fly.*

species, the "key" carried by the male will tend not to fit the female's "lock," which prevents her from receiving sperm that she is unable to use. In closely related species, it is more likely that the palp of one will fit the epigyne of another, but the likelihood of this happening is relatively remote, since the different courtship procedures of the two species means that the female will not accept the wrong male. Since each species of spider has its own unique palpal and epigynal structure, this has become an important diagnostic tool for their identification. However, these differences are not visible to the naked eye and cannot therefore be used for the identification of spiders in the field.

EVOLUTION OF THE PALPAL ORGAN

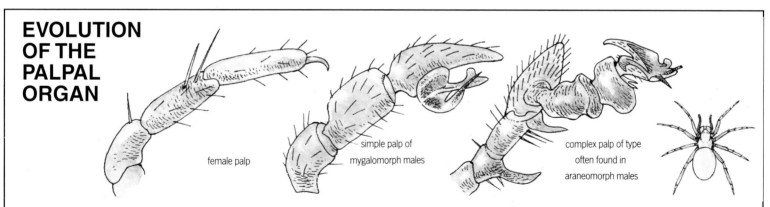

female palp

simple palp of mygalomorph males

complex palp of type often found in araneomorph males

The evolution of these structures in the spiders is unique within the arachnids, for within the other groups either the sperm is passed directly into the female from the male or a spermatophore is produced. It seems likely that the different course adopted by spiders was yet another way of overcoming the problem of the semen drying out if it was placed first on the ground

before being transferred to the female. The very earliest spiders probably simply transferred a drop of semen directly from their reproductive opening to that of the female by means of the tips of their then simple palps. It is then possible to visualize a series of steps whereby the end of the palp first enlarges and becomes cupshaped to accommodate more semen, and

this cup then becomes enclosed with just a narrow tube to the exterior to prevent the semen from being spilt. The whole structure, being very delicate, then evolved a protective sheath, the bulb, the whole being further protected by the enlarged tip of the palp in which it lies when not in use.

As these structures evolved individually in the different species

of spiders, so the epigyne of the female evolved to help guide the palp into the spermathecal ducts where the semen is deposited. The extreme complexity of knobs, spikes and spurs which exist on the palps of many male spiders today are probably of little use and are just there as ornamentation.

SENSE ORGANS

The only sense organs easily visible with the aid of a magnifying glass are the spider's eyes. Unlike the compound eyes of the insects, spiders have simple eyes which in eight-eyed spiders, the primitive condition, are arranged in two rows. We have already seen that in some spider families the number of eyes may be reduced, but they always occur in matching pairs. The arrangement of the rows as well as the number of eyes is used as a diagnostic tool in setting up spider families. In some cave-dwelling spiders, the eyes do not exist.

TASTE AND SMELL

Whether the senses of taste and smell are separate in spiders is debatable. We know that spiders are able to taste with the esophagus, for unpalatable food is quickly rejected, but they also possess a sense of "taste by touch" sited on the tips of the palps and legs. Tiny openings on the legs referred to as tarsal organs are also believed to be associated with taste and/or smell.

EYES

The eyes are of two types. "main eyes," always the center pair of the front row, possess a lens and a retina. These eyes are well developed in spiders that are active hunters; otherwise, they are small and are absent in the six-eyed spiders. The rest of the eyes are "secondary eyes," which also have a lens, but the retina differs from that of the main eyes in that the light-sensitive cells point away from the light (as they do in human eyes), rather than toward it. The majority of spiders do not depend at all on their eyesight for finding and capturing prey, and their sight is extremely poor.

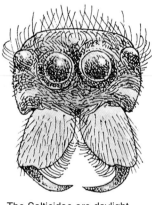

The Salticidae are daylight hunters with large eyes.

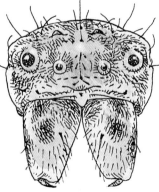

The Thomisidae are ambushers

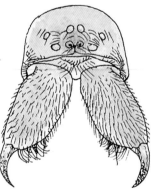

The Gnaphosidae are fierce nocturnal hunters with small eyes.

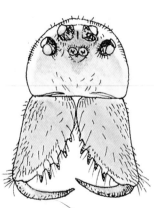

The Linyphiidae catch thier pray in webs so only have small eyes.

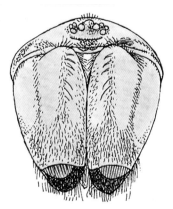

The Atpidae are mygalomorphs with huge jaws and small eyes

The Oonopidae usually have six eyes, but some species have only two.

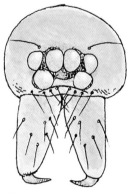

The Lycosidae are active daytime hunters with large eyes.

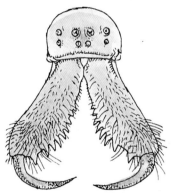

The Tetragnathidae are called big-jawed spiders, for obvious reasons.

SENSORY RECEPTORS

Spiders do not hear as such, but they do have a very well-developed ability to sense vibrations, both airborne and those transmitted through the surface on which they are standing. This sensory ability is sited in a number of different receptors spread around their body surface, but especially on the appendages. Structures called trichobothria are found on certain leg segments and consist of an upright hair set in a socket. The arrangement is somewhat like that of a gearshift in a car – the hair is able to move freely in all directions within the socket. Trichobothria respond to vibrations from moving insects; the way in which they move enables the spider to decide from which direction the insect is coming. Sensory hairs are found all over the body of the spider, and it has been found that only a single one needs to be touched in order to elicit an immediate response.

Spiders do respond to heat and cold, so they must also have temperature receptors on their body surface. Spiders are cold-blooded, and consequently they must maintain their body temperatures within necessary limits by

Some of the spider's sense organs are visible in the facial view (above) of a female salticid from Brazil's coastal rainforest. The eyes are obvious, but less so are the different types of sensitive hairs. Perhaps the most obvious of these are the trichobothria, the fine, dark, erect hairs projecting at intervals from the upper surface of the spider's legs.

means of behavioral patterns. In hot countries, they may hide from the heat of the sun during the day, or else align themselves at such an angle to the sun as to reduce the amount of heat falling upon them. In temperate countries they tend to seek the sun and may position themselves to obtain maximum exposure to it. During the cold months, they purposely seek out warm places under bark, in grass tufts or under leaf litter, where activity is kept to an absolute minimum.

COMMUNICATION

It may come as a surprise to learn that a number of spiders from different families communicate with each other by using sound, or at least what to us is sound, for spiders possess no ears as such. They do, however, have many vibration receptors on their body surface and since sound is vibration in the air we can assume that the spider "hears" this.

ACOUSTIC COMMUNICATION

Sound is most commonly produced by the file-and-scraper system, where one or more spines are scraped over a set of ridges. The name given to this kind of sound production, which is similar to that of grasshoppers and crickets, is stridulation.

Researchers have so far implicated acoustic communication in spiders in courtship, male-to-male aggression, and defense. An example of the latter may be found in certain theraphosid mygalomorph spiders which, when they are cornered, make a hissing sound by rubbing the palps on the jaws. The advantage of sound production in courtship becomes obvious when one considers the lifestyle of the spider. Any intruder into an individual spider's web or territory is possible prey, and failure to indicate that one is a potential mate could well end up in cannibalism. By making the correct noises, this danger can be avoided.

DRUMMING OUT THE MESSAGE

There are a number of ways in which a spider can produce sound.

1   It rubs its abdomen on its cephalothorax or on its waist.
2   It rubs one appendage against another: leg-leg, palp-leg, jaw-palp, or jaw-jaw.
3   It rubs an appendage against the abdomen.
4   It uses a file-and-scraper system on opposing parts of the same appendage.
5   It drums its palps or abdomen on the surface on which it is standing.
6   It vibrates one appendage against another.

Wolf spiders, (left) such as this pair of Pardosa amentata *in the author's backyard in England, have excellent eyesight and as a result much of their courtship is visual. The male waves his palps and front legs to the female in a characteristic display. He probably found her by her distinctive scent, and if she is frightened off, he will continue to stand and court thin air where she stood, an indication that he can still smell her presence there.*

Sound and vibrations are an important means of communication among spiders. For example, the male Araneus diadematus, (above) shown courting a rather large female, must first advise her of his good intentions by sending the correct set of vibrations through her web; otherwise, he could well end up as her meal rather than as her male.

CHEMICAL COMMUNICATION

The other form of communication known to exist in spiders is that by sex scents or pheromones. Pheromones are volatile chemicals secreted by spiders which enable them to determine the sex of any other spider that they meet or whose silk they come into contact with, for it seems that spider silk is coated with these substances as it is produced. In this way the male spider, for example, is able to find a female of his own species either by following her dragline or coming across her web.

SILK PRODUCTION

For most spiders, silk plays a major part in their everyday life. It is believed it evolved originally as a means of lining the burrow and then of protecting the eggs, either from drying out or from predators, or both. Only later did it also come to be used in the capture and wrapping of prey and the building of a lair.

Silk is produced by the abdominal silk glands, and at least seven different kinds are known to exist. Each gland produces its own kind of silk for a specific function.

Aciniform glands produce the silk for wrapping prey and are found in all spiders.

Cylindrical glands, silk from which is used by the female spider to protect the egg sac. Consequently, this type of gland is often absent in males, and it is also absent from members of the *Salticidate* and *Dysderidae* families.

HOW LONG IS A PIECE OF SILK?

Silk is a protein with amazing properties, for the strongest types have a breaking strain in excess of that of steel wire of the same diameter. Furthermore, silk can stretch to roughly double its length before it breaks. The silk that we see with the naked eye in fact consists of multiple single strands, each varying in thickness between about 10-6 in (3 x 10-5 mm) and approximately four times this diameter.

SPINNERETS

The type and arrangement of the spinnerets on the end of a spider's abdomen are important in deciding to which group or family it belongs. For example, the long, two-segmented pair of spinnerets in the family *Agelenidae* helps to distinguish it from members of the *Gnaphosidae*. Only seven spider families possess a cribellum that produces a special kind of trapping silk, the so-called "hackled band," in the manner shown in the diagram on the left. The cribellum is formed from a modified pair of spinnerets. As the silk is produced, it is combed out by the calamistrum, a row of special hairs situated on the metatarsus of each of the spider's hind legs.

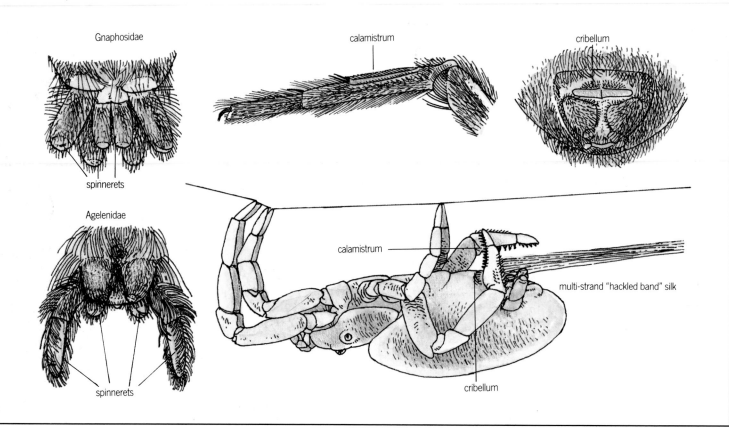

Gnaphosidae

calamistrum

cribellum

spinnerets

Agelenidae

calamistrum

multi-strand "hackled band" silk

spinnerets

cribellum

Ampullate glands – found in all spiders – are responsible for the production of the dragline, which all spiders leave behind as they move around.

Pyriform glands produce silk for the manufacture of attachment disks at the base of web-suspension lines, etc., and are found in all families.

Aggregate glands are restricted to three families, the *Araneidae*, *Theridiidae* and *Linyphiidae*, and produce the sticky droplets that are attached to the trapping lines of the web.

Lobed glands are found only in the *Theridiidae* and produce wrapping silk for this family. Consequently, the aciniform glands are much reduced.

Cribellar glands have been mentioned earlier (see page 21) as distinguishing the cribellate from the ecribellate spider families. These glands are numerous and secrete multistranded, slightly sticky silk through the many pores in the cribellum. This is then combed out with special hairs and combined with normal dragline silk to form the fluffy "hackled band" characteristic of the web of cribellate spiders. The fluffiness of this particular type of silk makes it ideal for trapping insects when the hairs on their legs become enmeshed in it.

No spider family possesses all seven types of gland, and it tends to be the web-building families that have the greatest profusion, for the wandering hunters have less need of silk. Equally, the male may have less well-developed glands than the female, for once he is mature, his only role is to seek out and mate with as many females as possible, a role where his need for silk is minimal.

Silk is produced as a liquid and is emitted from the spinnerets much as toothpaste is squeezed from a tube. It is believed that the liquid silk sets by the spider pulling on it; the harder the pull, the stronger the silk. As it oozes out and sets, the silk is manipulated by the highly mobile, fingerlike spinnerets into the marvellous handiwork associated with spiders.

Silk plays a very important role in a spider's life. For example, the female Cyrtophora hirta *(above) from Australia has used silk in making both her web and her elongated egg sac hanging in the background. The female orb-web spider* Argiope lobata *(right) from South Africa, on the other hand, is in the process of wrapping her grasshopper prey in silk.*

RECYCLING THE SILK

It is well known that spiders recycle their precious protein resources by eating their silk before they rebuild a web. The puzzle as to why spiderlings of the garden spider, *Araneus diadematus*, sometimes eat their webs before they need to rebuild has apparently been solved. When the webs were examined, it was found that they were often covered in pollen grains, which had adhered to the viscid silk of the spirals. This pollen serves as a source of food for the young spiders in the absence of insect prey, though it only provides a temporary respite, for they are unable to undergo a molt until they have consumed animal prey, an indication perhaps that vegetable food lacks some essential growth ingredient.

VENOMOUS SPIDERS

With the exception of one family, it is true to say that all spiders are venomous, but only a tiny proportion of them are capable of actually piercing human skin. Of those that can, many produce a painful bite, but only a very small proportion are actually dangerous to humans. There is no relationship between size and effect; for example, the bite of some of the largest mygalomorph tarantulas – though painful – produces few other effects. Deaths from spider bites are in fact quite rare and mainly occur in small children. Overall, they are much less harmful than scorpions, though the latter – being mainly nocturnal – are encountered less often than spiders.

DEADLY SPECIES

There are three genera of spiders whose bite is known to be deadly, all three from different spider families. Perhaps the best known of these is the black widow spider from the family *Theridiidae*. The black widow is represented by a number of species of *Latrodectus* from around the world, all of which are to some degree venomous. The common name black widow is derived from the misconception that the female always eats the male following mating, but this is not the case.

The species about which most is known is *Latrodectus mactans*, one of five species of this genus which occur in the U.S.A. They are not aggressive spiders and in fact are quite retiring. The author, for example, spent a good deal of time trying to photograph this species while on a trip to Mexico. He found plenty of webs, but when he approached, the spider usually rushed into its lair, and he eventually returned with just a single photograph of one in the wild. People usually get bitten by accident, for these spiders often live in close association with humans. They tend to end up in clothes or shoes, or in some position in which they can be squeezed against the skin, when a bite can occur. The same sort of problems occur with *Latrodectus hasselti* in Australia and *L. tredecimguttatus* in Europe. All three are shiny black spiders with red markings on the abdomen,

VENOMOUS SPIDERS

Depicted here is a selection of some of the world's more poisonous spiders. Although venomous spiders are found in many parts of the world, it is mainly children who are at risk from a fatal bite. In the U.S.A., for example, with several species of poisonous *Latrodectus*, and in Australia with its black widow and

funnel web mygalomorphs, the chance of being bitten by such a spider is roughly the same as that of being struck by lightning. The greatest number of recorded serious bites by spiders comes from the U.S.A., but this is probably a reflection of the understanding of what has occurred, both by the patient and by the doctor, rather than necessarily that these spiders are a threat to U.S. citizens. In the *(Continued overleaf)*

Southern black widow Latrodectus mactans, *female. (below left). The southern black widow spider is found in the West Indies and up the eastern side of North America from Mexico as far north as southern New England.*

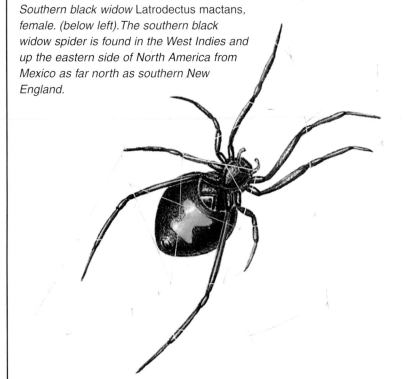

Western black widow Latrodectus hesperus, *male (below). The male of the western black widow from the southwest differs from the female, who resembles the southern black widow in being black with red marks beneath the abdomen.*

The notorious southern black widow spider (Latrodectus mactans) *(left), seen here in tropical Mexico, and its close relatives from the U.S.A., Europe and Australia, are implicated in many of the recorded spider bites in humans. They are, however, retiring creatures and only bite if provoked.*

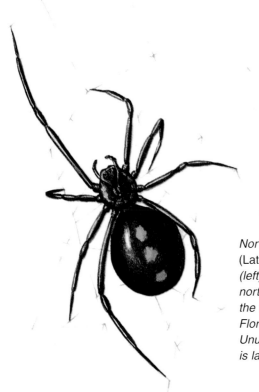

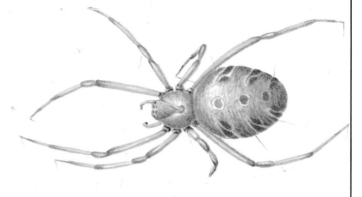

Northern black widow (Latrodectus variolus), *female (left). Despite its name, the northern black widow is found in the eastern states down into Florida and eastern Texas. Unusually for this genus, the male is larger than the female.*

Brown widow (Latrodectus geometricus) *female (above). The brown widow has a wide range, being found in many of the world's tropical regions, from where it has been introduced into, for example, southern Florida.*

and at one time they were considered to be a single species.

Some *Latrodectus* species, though still venomous, are not actually black. The brown widow, *L. geometricus*, a tropical species, is clearly brownish in color, while the beautiful red widow from Florida has a bright red to orange carapace and legs and black spotted abdomen with red and yellow markings.

The most obvious symptom of a black widow bite is the intense pain through the whole body which results from the venom attacking the nervous system. This attack can in turn lead to nausea, sickness, dizziness, profuse sweating, muscle spasms, and in some instances difficulties with breathing. Nowadays, as long as the patient is hospitalized as quickly as possible, deaths are rare, for antivenin injections are available to neutralize the effects of the toxins.

After the black widows, the next most notorious spiders are probably the Australian funnel web mygalomorph spiders of the genus *Atrax*. Unlike the retiring black widows, funnel web spiders, especially the wandering males, are extremely hostile and will attack when provoked. The Sydney funnel web *Atrax robustus* is, as its name implies, common around the suburbs of that city, though it has a fairly wide distribution southward

from there. As a city dweller, it is usually found in yards, where it often comes into contact with young children, and it is among them that the majority of deaths occur.

The effects of an attack are felt very quickly, with the site of the bite at first being very painful but soon going numb. The victim sweats profusely, nausea may be followed by vomiting, and they may collapse. This may be followed by breathing difficulties as a result of congestion in the lungs, with the victim turning blue as a result of oxygen shortage. Sharp cramping pains occur in the legs and abdomen, and the onset of delirium, muscular convulsions and finally coma may terminate in death.

The only other spiders of note which are highly venomous are wandering spiders of the genus *Phoneutria*. These creatures are found on the eastern side of South America and are especially common in some parts of Brazil, where they enter people's homes. They are quite large spiders, and their painful bites are again often fatal to young children.

OTHER HARMFUL BITERS
In the main, the other spiders venomous to man are less life-threatening or not at all, but the effects of their bites can be horrendous. One particularly

underdeveloped world of Central and South America, bites from poisonous spiders, especially among children, may be much more common since housing standards are much lower and provide a haven for these spiders. Also, young children are much less likely to understand what has bitten them, and doctors are much less freely available to diagnose the cause and to treat them. All in all, venomous spiders pose very much less of a threat to humans than scorpions and snakes, and with a little care and understanding of their habits, this threat could be reduced even more.

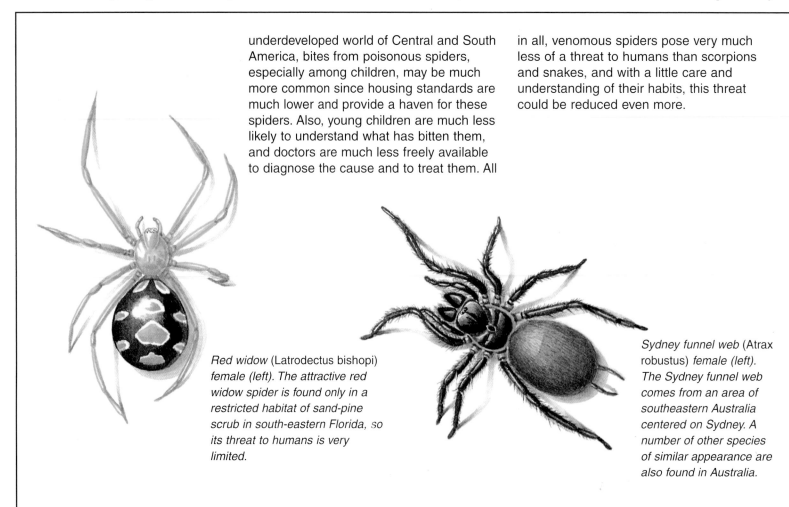

Red widow (Latrodectus bishopi) *female (left). The attractive red widow spider is found only in a restricted habitat of sand-pine scrub in south-eastern Florida, so its threat to humans is very limited.*

Sydney funnel web (Atrax robustus) *female (left). The Sydney funnel web comes from an area of southeastern Australia centered on Sydney. A number of other species of similar appearance are also found in Australia.*

unpleasant group of spiders with regard to the physical damage resulting from their bite are members of the genus *Loxosceles*, which have commonly become known as violin or brown spiders. The name violin spider comes from the violin-shaped mark on the carapace. The two species about which most is known of their effects on man are *L. laeta* from South America, whose bites can be fatal, and *L. reclusa* which is widespread in the Midwest. The symptoms of a bite from these two species, both of which tend to find their way into people's homes, are very similar. In most cases damage is restricted to the site of the bite and the surrounding area of tissue. Initially there is a small black spot, but this area of dead tissue gradually enlarges and deepens until it attains a diameter of as much as 6 in (150 mm). The ulcer can take up to four months to heal completely, and when it finally does, it leaves an unpleasant scar. Spiders of the worldwide genus *Chiracanthium* are quite small, but can also give a painful and potentially dangerous bite.

A VENOMOUS COCKTAIL

The venom from these spiders is a cocktail of mainly protein compounds, the main component which is common to all of them being alpha-latrotoxin. This venom is one of the most toxic substances known to man; for example, on a dry-weight basis, i.e., administering equal amounts of the dried venom to an experimental animal, it is 15 times as toxic as the poison of the prairie rattlesnake. We can be thankful, therefore, that these spiders are only small creatures and can inject but a tiny volume of poison. This is why the bite of the black widow seldom proves fatal to humans, and those deaths which do occur are often in very young children or in adults with heart disease or similar problems. U.S. data indicates that of those bites recorded over a period of 27 years during the earlier part of the 20th century, only 4 percent proved fatal. This is almost certainly much higher than the real figure, since many cases of black widow bites would not have been reported.

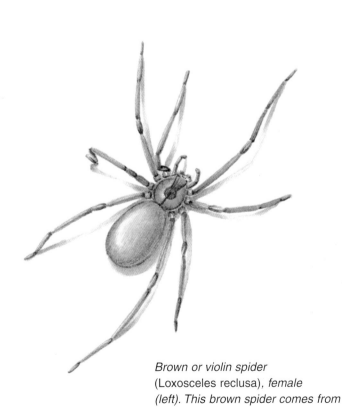

Brown or violin spider (Loxosceles reclusa), *female (left). This brown spider comes from the U.S. and has been introduced into Australia. It is one of about 50 species found around the world.*

Wandering spider (Phoneutria sp.), *female (right). Wandering spiders are found mainly in the hot countries of the world, but only* Phoneutria *from South America has so far been recorded as venomous to humans.*

SCORPIONS

Scorpions belong within the subclass *Scorpiones*. They are only very distantly related to spiders, a fact discussed earlier, and visually the only feature that they appear to have in common is the possession of four pairs of walking legs. In the scorpions, the legs are attached to the prosoma (cephalothorax), which bears on its upper surface a hard plate, the carapace. The prosoma is formed by fusion of the head and thorax and it bears the eyes, the jaws (chelicerae) and the pedipalps (palps) as well as the walking legs. Segmentation of the abdomen is absent in all but one primitive spider family, whereas that of scorpions is both clearly segmented and also divided into a broad mesosoma (preabdomen) and a long, narrow metasoma (postabdomen), at the tip of which is the telson (final segment) with its sting. The carapace may bear up to six pairs of eyes, one pair being placed roughly centrally while the others are sited at the corners of the front margin. Examination of the underside of the mesosoma reveals four pairs of spiracles, a pair on each segment, which open into the book lungs with which the animal breathes. On the hind segment is a pair of structures called pectines, which have a sensory function. Until recently, it was thought that they were used to detect the presence of prey or the unevenness of the ground on which they moved. Latest researches indicate that the male scorpion may use them to measure the size of the particles that make up the ground on which he is standing, for during courtship he prefers to find a surface made of small rather than large grains on which to deposit his spermatophore.

The telson contains two venom glands which empty out through a pair of tiny pores on each side of the sharp spine (aculeus) usually referred to as the sting. Muscles on the surface squeeze the glands against the hard inner wall of the telson, which forces the venom out through the sting.

COURTSHIP

There is relatively little variation in the courtship of scorpions. Since both sexes are nocturnal and only emerge from their burrows at night, they find each other by scent, vibration, and touch. Having found one another, the male then usually grasps the female's palps in his pincers and proceeds to dance with her. This dance, which may last from several hours to reportedly several days in some species, involves a random backward, forward and sideways movement of the two animals over the ground. The males do not always hold the females, for in a number of species the two just move in time, face to face, without actually touching each other. As the pair dance, they may also hold the thin part of the abdomen up in the air so that their stings are in contact. It seems that the role of this activity is to find a suitably fine-grained surface upon which the male can deposit his spermatophore.

Once the pair have found a suitable site, the male then deposits the spermatophore, a fairly complex substance, only a small volume of which actually consists of spermatozoa. The spermatophore adheres to the ground by a special sticky pad, the holdfast. The mating process itself involves the male maneuvering the female into position, so that her reproductive opening is over the spermatophore. In the correct position, the female's underside catches on the hooks on the spermatophore, pulling it apart and directing the semen into her body.

SCORPIONS AND THEIR PREY

Scorpions mainly feed on other arthropods, though some of the larger species have been recorded as taking lizards and small snakes on occasions; cannibalism occurs occasionally. The scorpion uses its jaws to break the prey up into particles, which are then packed into and held between the bottom segments (coxae) of the palps. Digestive juices from the mouth (buccal cavity) are then poured onto them. This converts the food into a liquid, which the scorpion squeezes out with the bottom segments of its jaws and swallows. The sucked-out remains of the prey are then rejected as a small pellet. The structure and function of the alimentary canal and the way in which waste products are removed from the body are much the same as for the spiders.

This intimidating creature (opposite) is a scorpion of the genus Pandinus *out hunting for prey at night in temperate South African rainforest. Some of its close relations reach as much as 8 in (200 mm) from head to sting, though this one is somewhat smaller, around 4 in (100 mm) in length. Scorpions are most likely to be encountered on the ground, but some, like this one, will also climb into trees and shrubs in seach of a meal. When it encounters prey animals, it grasps them in its large pincers, tears them apart and chews them up, bit by bit, with its jaws, which are just visible here protruding from the front of the head end. Only if the prey is large and unmanageable will the scorpion bring its sting into action. Although the scorpion seems to be peering up at the observer with the pair of main eyes on top of its head, these cannot actually form images and are there to tell the scorpion the difference between light and dark.*

LIFE CYCLE

Although the scorpions are divided up into a number of families, there is very little difference to be found between them in terms of their life cycle. Whereas all spiders produce eggs, no scorpions do so directly, for the eggs are fertilized and retained within the female's body, where development takes place. Some species of scorpion produce eggs rich in yolk, which supplies all of the nutrients necessary for development of the young within the mother's body, a phenomenon known as ovoviviparity. In other species, however, the eggs contain only a small amount of yolk. The remaining food that the young need is obtained directly from the female's body, an example of viviparity. Parthenogenesis is known to occur in the Brazilian species *Tityus serratulus*.

As soon as the young scorpions leave their mother's body they clamber onto her back, where they remain for up to two weeks. At first they are very pale, but on contact with the air their outer layers gradually develop their normal color. During the time they spend on her back, their mother does not feed them, but she does protect them. They finally undergo a molt, by which time the yolk that has nourished them since they hatched has been used up, and they leave their mother and begin to catch their own prey.

SCORPION AS HUNTER

Scorpions spend the day in their burrow and leave it at night to hunt. The majority of them are desert or semidesert dwellers, and the burrow acts as a refuge from the hot, dry conditions of such habitats. Scorpions apparently use at least two methods to dig. Some loosen the soil with their jaws and then use the front pair of legs to scoop the soil out. The alternative method is well described for the South African species *Cheloctonus jonesii*.

This scorpion has been seen to drag its sensory feelers over a large surface area of soil in an apparent search for a suitable place in which to dig, which adds further substance to the theory that they act as mechanoreceptors for testing soil texture. It excavates a vertical burrow which seems to act as a pitfall trap, for the remains of various ground-dwelling beetles have been found at the bottom of the shaft. *C. jonesii* uses the lobsterlike claws on its palps to loosen the soil, using what is effectively a digging action. At first, the palps are used alternately; but as the burrow develops, they are used together. The palps are also used to remove the soil, with the scorpion holding it against the underside of its thorax with them while it backs out of the burrow. Once out, it turns around and deposits the soil a short distance from the burrow entrance.

Scorpions are able to regulate their body temperature by retreating to the depths of their burrows in the hottest part of the day, when the upper layers of soil are very hot. As night comes, the scorpions emerge onto the surface to hunt. The time they spend there varies from species to species, but in general, as time progresses and the surface temperatures fall, they make their way back into their burrows, where they can benefit from the heat still locked up in the soil from the previous hours of sunlight.

Since scorpions are either exclusively nocturnal or, in the dark depths of the tropical forest diurnal, there is no evidence of their use of camouflage or mimicry. They do, however, have enemies, which include a range of insectivorous birds and mammals that have learned how to avoid their

VENOMOUS SCORPIONS

Of the 1200 or so species of scorpions presently known to humans, only about 50 are dangerously venomous to us. What is interesting is that there is no relationship between size and effect, and indeed it is often the smaller species that are the most harmful.

Because young children are smaller than adults, they are much more seriously affected by scorpion bites: in Trinidad the mortality rate from stings was reported as 25 percent in children but only 0.25 percent in adults; similarly in Brazil, deaths from *Tityus serratulus* have been reported as 1 percent in adults, 3–5 per cent in schoolchildren and 15–20 percent in very young children. In the state of Guerrero in Mexico, in the years 1970–1974, 6 percent of deaths in children under the age of 5 were attributed to scorpion stings, an indication of just how venomous they are. The majority of stings in the U.S.A. are caused by *Centruroides sculpturatus*, a species which occurs in Arizona along with the black widow spider, which is considered to be much less dangerous.

In mild cases of scorpion envenomation, effects may include local swelling, pain and discoloration at the site of the sting, which may be accompanied by fever and occasionally nausea and vomiting. Such symptoms usually subside within about 24 hours of being stung. In more severe cases, the following symptoms are common in patients stung by a number of unrelated venomous species from around the world:

1 Anxiety and agitation.
2 Severe pain at the site of the sting.
3 Excessive salivation and perspiration.
4 An irregular pulse accompanied by an unstable body temperature.
5 Breathing difficulties.
6 Muscular twitching, which may in its extreme form lead to convulsions and finally death.
Post-mortem examination of these patients often reveals some damage to both the heart and lungs.

sting. In the study of *Cheloctonus jonesii*, it was found that its predators included lesser red musk shrews, two species of hornbill and the bushveld gerbil. Centipedes also seem to be important predators of scorpions, for species of the genus *Scolopendra* took *C. jonesii* in South Africa.

The sting, which scorpions use to immobilize large prey, shows up clearly at the tip of the abdomen of this Parabuthus sp. *from southern Africa. Although not deadly, its sting is very painful to humans. Much of the volume of the last segment, from which the sting protrudes, is occupied by two sacs filled with venom.*

THE DESERT ARACHNIDS

Deserts and semideserts such as are found in the southwest and over much of Mexico contain a great wealth of animal life, much of which is nocturnal and therefore seldom seen. These areas also contain a great variety of plants. Some, like the cacti, the agaves, the yuccas and the creosote bush, are present all year round. Others temporarily cover the desert after the annual rains. Together these plants provide a source of food for the many desert insects, which in turn provide food for the arachnids. The situation here is not quite true to life, for although the grasshopper and the mites might be spotted during the day, the others would only be seen by flashlight at night. They have all been depicted in a daylight scene so that they can be seen in their true colors. The pair of *Centruroides* scorpions **(1)** are busily engaged in a courtship dance, while the "tarantula" *Brachypelma* **(2)** is about to pounce on the sleeping grasshopper, which it may eventually reject, as grasshoppers are highly distasteful. The whip scorpion **(3)** is climbing the cactus in search of prey, which it will immobilize and kill with the impressive array of spikes on its front appendages. The *Trombidiid* mites **(4)** are only a few millimeters long and wander around looking for even tinier arthropods on which to feed.

Scale

1 *Centruroides* scorpions, 2 in (50 mm).

2 *Brachypelma*, 1½ in (40 mm)

3 Whip scorpion, 2 in (50 mm).

4 *Trombidiid* mites, ¹⁄₁₀ in (3 mm)

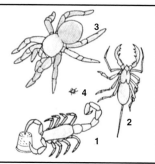

OTHER ARACHNID GROUPS

THE MITES AND TICKS (SUBORDER *ACARI*)

It is likely that the 20,000 species of this group that have so far been described represent only a small fraction of the number ever likely to be found, for many of them are microscopic. This is one of the arachnid groups in which head, thorax, and abdomen are fused into a single structure. Although the majority are free-living, both on land and in water, they have gained notoriety because a number of them are parasites of man and his domestic animals, and apart from the direct effects of their blood-sucking activities, they can also transmit some very unpleasant diseases. Some species, such as the red spider mite (which is actually yellow, but appears red in massed groups), are parasites upon cultivated plants, where they can cause considerable economic damage. The ticks are separated from the mites by their greater size and the fact that all ticks are parasites.

One unpleasant characteristic of the ticks is the way in which their bodies can inflate greatly when they feed on the blood of their host. On the plus side, some mites are actually useful to man. The follicle mite, for example, is to be found in human hair follicles and sebaceous glands, where it helps to keep the skin clean. The house mite, although a problem to some people, in whom it can induce asthmalike

Harvestmen like this Phalangium opilio *(left) from Europe are often mistaken for spiders, but a close look soon reveals the differences in body arrangement. The red Trombidiid mites (top) floating on the surface of a rock pool on the Kenyan coast, along with a group of springtails, maybe found on almost any shore.*

symptoms, is useful in that it feeds on dead skin cells and other matter which would otherwise accumulate in the house. In common with most of the other suborders in the *Arachnida*, the mites and ticks are fluid feeders. The group has a worldwide distribution.

THE HARVESTMEN (SUBORDER *OPIOLINES*)

Like the mites and ticks, the harvestmen have the head, thorax and abdomen fused into a single structure, but that is as far as the similarity goes, for the latter are free-living predators upon other arthropods. They often, but not always, have legs which can be up to 30 times the length of the body. (Mites and ticks have very short legs.) Body size of most harvestmen lies in the range 0.25–0.5 in (6–12 mm).

They are the group most likely to be confused with the spiders, but they may be distinguished from the latter by the fused cephalothorax and abdomen and by the fact that the abdomen shows clear segmentation, a characteristic found only in the rarely seen, primitive liphistiid spiders.

Harvestmen are omnivorous in nature, living on small arthropods, dead or alive, as well as fungus and plant material. Digestion is internal, and some solid food is taken in, something that is uncharacteristic of arachnids. The male possesses a penis with which he introduces sperm into the female's reproductive opening, and she then lays her eggs in cracks and crevices around her with the assistance of her ovipositor. They have a worldwide distribution, though those from the tropics tend to be shorter-legged than temperate species.

PSEUDOSCORPIONS (SUBORDER *PSEUDOSCORPIONES*)

These creatures are given the name pseudo- or false scorpions on account of their superficial resemblance to scorpions. Like the scorpions they have enlarged palps bearing pincers at the ends with which they grasp their prey; but unlike the scorpions, the abdomen is short and rounded and lacks a terminal sting. Most pseudoscorpions are only just visible with the naked eye, the largest being no more than about 0.25 in (6 mm) long, with the majority of species only half this size. They may be found under stones, in moss, in leaf litter, under bark, in insect nests, in caves and even in human homes, where they feed upon tiny insects and their larvae. A few species hitch rides on other arthropods, seemingly to move from one environment to another. They trap prey with the pincers on the ends of their palps and then immobilize it by injecting it with poison from their jaws. The venom comes not from the tip of the fang, as it does in spiders, but from the immovable base of the jaw, which injects venom into the prey when the prey is pulled against it. Digestion is external and the liquid formed is then sucked into the gut.

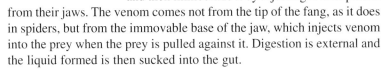

Pseudoscorpions share with spiders the ability to make silk, which is used to build a secure hideaway, either during molting or by the female when she is swollen with eggs and vulnerable. The spinnerets are located not on the abdomen, as they are in the spiders, but on the jaws. Courtship is similar to that of scorpions, the pair performing a dance until the male finds a suitable place to deposit his spermatophore. He then leaves and the female moves over the spermatophore and takes the sperm mass up into her reproductive opening. In common with the scorpions, the young develop in a transparent envelope on the underside of the female's abdomen. On hatching, the larvae are initially fed on a secretion from the ovary, but after molting they become active and disperse. Pseudoscorpions have a worldwide distribution.

TAILED WHIP SCORPIONS (SUBORDER *UROPYGI*)

As their name implies, these animals bear a superficial resemblance to the scorpions, but the hindmost abdominal segments are slender, forming a whiplike tail (hence their name), but lack a sting at the tip. The palps are large and are used for grasping and immobilizing (they lack the venom glands of spiders) their mainly insect prey, which is then chewed up with the jaws. The largest species, which may grow up to 3 in (75 mm) long, is found in the southern U.S.A., where it is often referred to by the common name of vinegaroon or vinagrillo. This name is derived from its ability to squirt from its abdomen a mixture of organic acids, including ethanoic acid (vinegar). The pungent acid spray is used by the vinegaroon to ward off attack by lizards and other small vertebrate enemies. The majority of species are tropical in distribution.

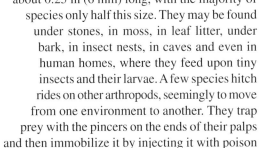

TAILLESS WHIP SCORPIONS (SUBORDER *AMBLYPYGI*)

These animals somewhat resemble the previous group, but they are much flattened and lack the tail whip; the first pair of walking legs is extremely thin and elongated, and the carapace is broader than it is long. They hunt at night over tree trunks and the surface of rocks, and if threatened they are able to move off at high speed, their flattened body allowing them to hide under bark and in crevices or similar places.

Their palps are extremely spiny, enabling them to catch, crush and pierce their prey with great efficiency before breaking it up with their jaws. They are mainly tropical in distribution, though at least three species are recorded from the southern half of the U.S.A., two from Florida and one from Arizona.

SUN SPIDERS (SUBORDER *SOLIFUGAE*)

At first sight, these animals resemble spiders, but unlike the spiders their abdomen is clearly segmented. The larger species, which may attain a length of 2.5 in (64 mm), appear to be quite intimidating, with their noticeably large jaws accounting for nearly one-third of their total body length. They lack poison glands, however, and are unable to maneuver them effectively to pierce human skin, except on rare occasions, when the bite has been described as painful but that is all. Instances of so-called "poisoning" by sun spiders is almost certainly a result of secondary bacterial infection of the wound.

In the main, the solifugids are denizens of the world's deserts, and indeed their presence in an area is an indicator of desert conditions. They are, however, absent from the deserts of Australia, nor are they found in New Zealand or Madagascar. They require warmth, though at least one species has been recorded at an altitude of 10,000 ft (3000 m) in the Pamir Mountains of Asia. In addition to being called sun spiders they are also called false spiders, wind scorpions, wind spiders and a number of other common names relating either to their love of warmth or the speed at which they can move. The Afrikaans name "haarskeerder," in English "haircutter," comes from the erroneous belief that, should a solifugid become entangled in a girl's long hair, it cannot be removed until it has cut itself free with its huge jaws.

Solifugids spend the daylight hours in burrows which may extend a considerable depth into the earth and may be several yards long. In the hottest times of the year, they go deep into their burrows, but in cooler, damper conditions they may be found near the entrance. The individuals of some species have been recorded as digging more than 40 burrows during their lifetime.

They are primarily nocturnal although a few of the smaller species, some of which are brightly colored, are active during the day, giving rise to their common name, sun spiders. They are well adapted to life in the desert, being able to withstand higher temperatures for longer periods of time than other desert arthropods; the rate at which they lose water through the body surface is also very low.

Some solifugids run actively over the ground or across trees and shrubs in search of their prey, which like many arachnids they find by vibration and touch. The climbing species may be aided by the suckers on the palps, with which they are able to hold onto whatever surface they are on. Others stalk their prey, especially where it may be present in large numbers, for example around nests of termites, the food of most North American solifugids. In Texas, two species of *Eremobates* commonly enter human homes to hunt, possibly drawn by light. A number of African desert species seem to be attracted to the light of campfires, where they feed upon insects which have also been lured there by the light. The larger species have also been seen to take scorpions and large spiders as well as vertebrate prey in the form of lizards, small rodents and birds. Solifugids are very aggressive toward one another, and ferocious fights may result in the eventual death of one of the combatants, who then provides a meal for the victor.

Prey is broken up mechanically by the huge jaws, and the liquid contents are sucked into the alimentary canal, with digestion occurring internally rather than externally, as in the true spiders. Solifugids have been seen to take a drink when water is available, but being desert dwellers they probably obtain most of their water requirements from their food.

The male uses his jaws to transfer sperm, which he has first released onto the ground, into the female's reproductive opening. Alternatively, the sperm may be transferred directly into the female, the jaws being used to complete this insertion process. The female then constructs a burrow in which she lays her eggs. The eggs are then abandoned by the female, or in some species she remains with them until they hatch and then protects

Tailless whip scorpions, like this one (above) from the Shimba Hills in Kenya, are flattened in shape so that they can scuttle into narrow gaps under bark and between rocks to escape their enemies. Sun spiders (solifugids), on the other hand, are quite robust creatures, as can be seen from this South African Solpuga *(top right). It could be mistaken for a spider, but the leglike palps and the segmented abdomen make it apparent that it is not. Many solpugids are nocturnal, but this one is active in daytime.*

Unlike their close relations the spiders, sun spiders do not produce poison to kill their prey, but use their enormous jaws (right) instead. The photographer was also able to observe the jaws of a female of this southern African species being put to another use, that of cutting into the earth during burrow construction. Having loosened some earth with her jaws, she held her palps in front of her and, in the manner of a bulldozer, pushed the soil away from the burrow.

them until they are ready to disperse. Unlike other larger arachnids, such as scorpions and mygalomorph spiders, solifugids are not long-lived, one year being their normal lifespan. Sun spiders occur in their greatest profusion in Africa and the Near East, though 100 species are known in the U.S.A., mainly from the warm southwest.

COURTSHIP AND MATING

Since in most spider species the sexes lead independent lives, when the mating season arrives there has to be some way in which they can get together for the purposes of courtship and mating. This usually involves the males starting out on a search for females, but before they do so one important function has to be carried out, that of sperm induction, i.e., the charging of the palpal organs with semen.

The male of the European Meta segmentata *is about to mate with the female while she is engrossed in eating a fly that she has just captured and wrapped in silk.*

THE SEARCH FOR A MATE

It would be physically possible for many male spiders to place the palpal organ against their genital opening and fill it with semen directly, but this is not known to occur in any species. Instead the male produces a special sperm web onto which he deposits a drop of semen, which is then taken up into the palpal organ. In its simplest form, the sperm web consists of a single strand of silk held between one pair of legs and upon which a droplet of semen is deposited. In more advanced species, the sperm web is spun in a quadrangular or triangular shape. Semen is deposited on one side of the web and is then drawn into the palps from the opposite side. Despite the tiny volumes involved, sperm induction takes a considerable time, anything between 30 minutes in most spiders and three to four hours in some mygalomorphs.

Having charged his palpal organs, the male now feels the urge to find a mate. In some species, where males and females live in close proximity within the same environment, this may mean moving only a short distance, while in others the males may have to travel much farther. It is a fact that the only time when many of the trapdoor spiders are likely to be seen, without digging them up, is when the males are wandering in search of females. Any small animal that moves around

CHARGING THE PALPAL ORGAN

In order for the male to charge his palpal organ with sperm, he first constructs a tiny sperm web. He – in this instance an *Araneus* orbweb male – then squeezes a tiny drop of semen onto the web from his genital opening, and sucks it up into his palpal organ.

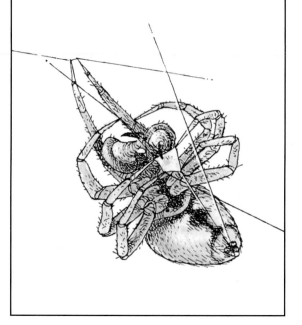

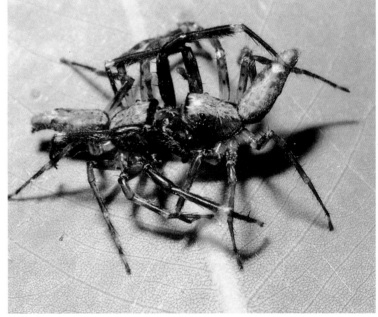

The complex male palpal organs are clearly visible on the Peucetia sp. lynx spider (far left) from Mexico. The tiny male of Nephila clavipes (left) from Central America wanders around unmolested in the female's web and can mate with her at will. Some male spiders, such as the tiny male salticids Helpis minitabunda (below) from Australia, will fight quite ferociously over a female.

is vulnerable to attack by predators, and this is the case with spiders. Since a single male can mate with more than one female, the loss of a few males as they wander around looking for females is relatively unimportant. The loss of even a single female, however, would mean the loss of a whole set of offspring in the eggs that she would fail to lay, something that the species can ill afford.

We know that as spiders move around they leave behind them a silken dragline, and that the one the female spins is covered in her own particular sexual scent or pheromone. Thus, once a male spider comes into contact with the female's dragline, he is able to recognize it and follow it until he finds her. This is probably the main way in which free-living spiders find their mates, though in big-eyed families, such as the jumping spiders, vision may play a part. A web-building female spider also coats her silk with scent so that the male can recognize her web when he comes across it. The male fishing spider, *Dolomedes triton*, begins his courtship only when he comes across an area of pond surface which has recently been occupied by a female. It is believed that he is activated by scent, from the female's cuticle, which dissolves in the water.

COURTSHIP RITUALS

Courting begins once the male has found a female of his own species. There is a great deal of variation in the amount of courtship that is required before mating takes place, but in all instances the female must first recognize that the object that is approaching her is a courting male and not prey. Second, her natural predatory instincts have to be switched off in some way before she can become switched on by her suitor's attentions. If these female instincts are not suppressed, the male spider is likely to end up as a meal rather than a mate. It is the pattern of courtship that makes sure that these two points are satisfied.

In some spiders the pregnant female is sufficiently subdued for the male to be able to walk up to her and mate with the minimum of courtship. Alternatively, the male may move in with her until she becomes mature, whereupon mating takes place without any complex courtship. In most spiders, however, something more than this is needed before the female will accept the male as a mate. It is not possible in the limited space available to describe all of the courtship ploys used by male spiders – they would take a book on their own – but a few examples will suffice to show just how complex and interesting they can be.

VISUAL SIGNALS

In the long-sighted hunters, such as the salticids and the wolf spiders, courtship is very much a visual process, and although the male may in the first instance discover the female's whereabouts from her scent, once he is fairly close to her he can probably recognize her visually. We know that the females leave a scent behind them, for a male will continue to court the spot from which his prospective mate has recently departed. Once the male spider is in range of the female, he may begin a series of movements, waving his legs and/or palps. These act as a signal to the female, informing her of his amorous intentions and letting her know that he is not potential prey. To this end, many male salticids have beautifully marked and colored palps, each pattern unique to his particular species. The combination of different signals and different palpal patterns means that a female will recognize and mate with a male of her own species and not with one of another. Having accepted the presence of the male, she allows him to approach, but it may require a good deal of stroking and caressing by the male before actual mating occurs.

Interestingly, in a number of species, the male has complex ornamentation even though there is seemingly no longer any visual courtship, this apparently having been lost with time.

PHYSICAL CONTACT

In mygalomorphs and the short-sighted hunting spiders, much of the courtship involves touch, the correct sequence of strokes and caresses being sufficient for the female to allow the male to mate with her. The male in a number of the crab spiders is considerably smaller than the female and as such is generally ignored by her. He thus has no problem in crawling beneath her body and mating with her.

Much more interesting is the behaviour of the male of the *Xysticus* crab spiders prior to mating. Upon finding a female, he walks up to her and grasps the femur of one of her front legs in his jaws. This provokes an immediate attack response from her which, held as she is, is not normally

---

VISUAL COURTSHIP IN LONG-SIGHTED SPIDERS

With their large and efficient eyes, jumping spiders have evolved a visual courtship routine during which the female comes to accept the presence of the male as a prospective mate rather than as prey. In this sequence the male is signaling by waving his front legs from side to side, while at the same time trotting sideways. He repeats this movement until the female is ready to accept him.

The male wolf spider is also indulging in visual courtship, raising and lowering his velvety black palps alternately, at the same time vibrating them and his front legs so violently that it is possible to see them with the naked eye, despite his diminutive size.

The male of the European wolf spider Pardosa amentata *displays to the female with his black palps, raising first one and then the other at an angle of 45° to the side of his head. In this particular instance, the female has departed, frightened off by the presence of the photographer. The male, however, appears to be made of sterner stuff, for he continues to display doggedly to the site where she originally stood.*

successful, as the male holds onto his advantage. Once she has quietened down, he climbs on to her back and circles around, stroking her gently with his legs. Not only does this make the female more submissive, but it also allows him to weave a silken halter around her head and legs, effectively tying her to the surface on which she is perched. Once she is firmly anchored, the male is able to lift her abdomen and mate with her, an act which can take an hour and a half. After he has left her, having completed his task, the female is easily able to break free from her bonds and resume her daily rounds.

Until fairly recently, this restricting of the female's movements by the use of silk was only known from the above example, but we now know that another spider uses a similar technique. The male of the fisher spider, *Pisaurina mira*, uses silk to tie together his mate's front two pairs of legs. He then firmly holds her other two pairs in his legs while he mates with her. Once again, the female can break free of her bonds very easily once mating is over.

SOUND

Certain male spiders make use of sound during courtship. The male of *Lycosa gulosa*, a wolf spider common in grassland in the U.S.A., produces sound percussively by rapidly drumming his palps upon the surface on which he is standing. When a captive male drums on the resonant floor of his cage, the noise he makes is clearly audible. Since he is a ground-dwelling animal, it is probable that the "noise" he produces in courtship is actually in the form of vibrations transmitted through the ground to his mate.

The European "buzzing spider," *Anyphaena accentuata*, is well named, for in his case the sound made by the male is audible in the wild, though once again it is likely that the female detects only vibrations rather than sounds. This species is a tree dweller, and the male usually finds a prospective mate sitting on a leaf. During the courtship, he vibrates his abdomen rapidly against the surface of the leaf, producing the characteristic buzzing sound.

More recently, it has been found that a number of jumping spiders from around the world also produce sounds during courtship. In Australia, for example, there is a species of jumping spider which produces so much sound that it was mistakenly thought, at first, to be a calling cricket. The spider in question, *Saitis michaelseni*, bears a pair of files on the posterior surface of the cephalothorax, and on the opposing face of the abdomen there is an area of short hairs with a bulbous base; these structures are present only in the males. Sound is emitted when it rubs the abdominal hairs over the file on its cephalothorax.

As with the other two species mentioned, acoustic communication is only used once the male has found a female. During courtship, which usually takes place on the surface of dry, fallen leaves in the ground-leaf litter, the male first signals visually to the female, whom he inevitably finds on the lower surface of the leaf. This visual display finds the male moving his white-tipped first pair of legs up and down in front of his mate. He then moves to the upper surface of the leaf and stands with the female exactly below him on the lower surface. Here he produces short bursts of sound every few seconds. This first phase is followed by a second phase when longer bursts of sound occur with longer intervals in between.

NUPTIAL FEEDING

In one pisaurid wolf spider, *Pisaura mirabilis*, there is a courtship act unique among spiders, that of nuptial feeding (shown below). However, recent research into this species in captivity has shed a different light upon the role of the nuptial gift. Ever since this specific behavior pattern was first recognized, it was translated as an attempt by the male to prevent himself from being cannibalized by his mate. We now know that this is not apparently the case, for when captive pairs of *Pisaura* were kept together for several days after mating had taken place in the laboratory, the female never ate the male. What is even more interesting is that the only times that cannibalism was observed, once when a male ate a female and twice when females ate males, the factor which initiated it was a fight over the nuptial gift.

So why does the male *Pisaura* present his mate with a captured insect? It would seem that the answer relates to mate selection by the female. In the first instance, she will not allow a male without a gift to mate with her at all; and second, the larger the gift and the longer she takes to feed on it, the longer the male has to introduce his sperm into her. Add to this the fact that the nuptial gift supplies extra food for the development of her eggs and the reason for the behavior can immediately be appreciated. This, however, leads to another question: why has nuptial feeding not evolved in other species? There are two possible answers. The first is that the evolution of what is in fact a very complicated behavior pattern requires a whole set of circumstances to be met, and the likelihood of these occurring together is very remote. The second is that we know very little about the behavior of most of the world's spiders, and it may be that nuptial feeding does occur in other species.

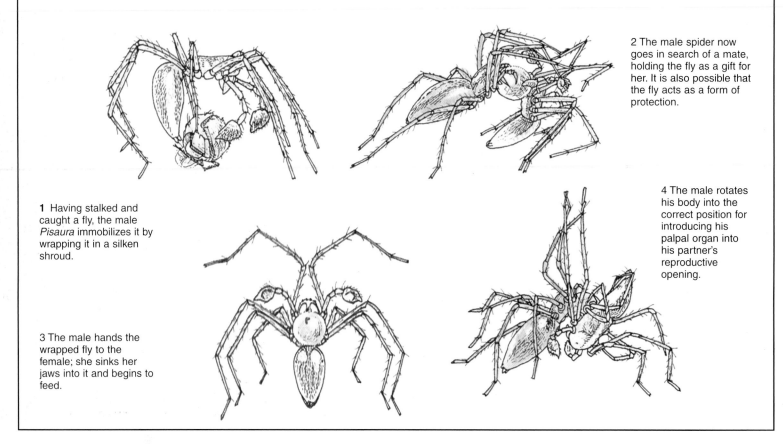

1 Having stalked and caught a fly, the male *Pisaura* immobilizes it by wrapping it in a silken shroud.

2 The male spider now goes in search of a mate, holding the fly as a gift for her. It is also possible that the fly acts as a form of protection.

3 The male hands the wrapped fly to the female; she sinks her jaws into it and begins to feed.

4 The male rotates his body into the correct position for introducing his palpal organ into his partner's reproductive opening.

Finally, he moves beneath the leaf where he uses a combination of this rubbing sound, visual signaling and percussive sound (by striking his first pair of legs on the leaf) before finally making contact with the female prior to mating.

It is the approach of a male to the female on a web that is fraught with the most danger, since any vibration she normally detects is likely to be interpreted as the presence of a potential meal. Males of these kinds of spiders have a repertoire of signals which they send through the web to indicate to the female who they are and what they intend. Unlike the irregular vibrations sent by a trapped insect, these have a particular pattern so that she may easily recognize them. In spiders with a suspended web, the male usually has a dragline behind him; if the female attacks, he can let go and drop away from her.

AMPHIBIOUS COURTSHIP

Instead of sending vibrations through the air or ground, the male *Dolomedes* sends messages across the surface of the water on which he hunts by jerking his abdomen up and down in a regular rhythm. This results in uniformly spaced waves spreading across the water, which presumably the female spider is able to distinguish from the uneven waves produced by insect prey that, for example, have fallen in and are struggling on the surface. He then follows her dragline across plants on the water surface, or by rowing and pulling if it happens to run across the water at any point, until he finds her. There then follows a prolonged period of leg-play between them before mating takes place.

Spiders of the genus Dolomedes *spend most of their lives on or near the surface of lakes and ponds. They pick up information from the water surface about members of the opposite sex whose pheromones are being dispersed across the water surface. Here (below left) a juvenile* Dolomedes fimbriatus *is dipping its front legs into the water to pick up any vibrations which might be of interest to it.*

The small males of Argiope bruennichi *are in grave danger from their large mates (below right), who wrap them in silk during mating.*

THE DANGERS OF COURTSHIP

It is a fact of life that the male spider often ends up as a meal for the female once mating is completed, especially in those species where he is considerably smaller than his mate. As long as he has already mated, this is not really any loss to him; for once the mating season is over, his days are numbered and he will die anyway. As a meal for the female, he supplies precious nutrients for the development of the eggs within her body and the eventual production of his offspring, the reason he mated with her in the first place.

The danger to which the male web-builder is exposed in his courtship of the female varies very much from family to family and from species to species within a family. In the *Agelenidae*, where the males are not much smaller than the females, courtship tends to be short and sweet, and as long as she is receptive, the female will allow the male to mate without any fuss. Females of the theridiid *Steatoda bipunctata*, a "domestic" species associated with human habitation both in Europe and the U.S.A. (where it has been introduced) actually signal to their males their presence in the web. The male first starts courtship by entering the female's web, where he indicates his presence by walking jerkily around. She then plucks the web in response, thus indicating that she is at home and prepared to receive him.

Courtship in araneids varies from the sublime to the ridiculous with regard to the way in which the male is received. In the very large, tropical, orb-web spiders of the genus *Nephila*, the female is usually many times bigger than the male, up to 1000 times his weight in some instances. Because of this enormous discrepancy in size, the male is below the female's prey size threshold; to put it another way, if she bothered to attack and kill him he would not even make a mouthful. As a result, the male is able to walk around in her web unmolested and mate with her at will. Much the same is true of members of the genus *Argiope*, though here the difference in size of the sexes is not quite so marked. During mating in the European *Argiope bruennichi*, however, all is not as affable as it seems, for as he

Males of Araneus *spiders are often in grave danger of being eaten by their considerably larger mates if courtship and mating are not undertaken with some care. The male European A. quadratus (left), on the right of the picture, is sharing the female's lair until she molts into adulthood, when he will mate with her before her jaws harden. At the moment, she is not much bigger than he is, so he is in little danger from her, but this will not be the case once she is mature.*

An alternative method (right) is so far known only from this European crab spider, Xysticus cristatus, *and from an American pisaurid. The darker-colored male, bending over the abdomen of the paler female and mating with her, has tied her down with silk to keep her immobile. Interestingly, this does not substantially reduce the danger that he might be in, for after mating she has no trouble at all in pulling herself free of her bonds.*

is inserting his first palp the female gently binds him in silk. Having emptied the first palp, he then inserts the second, after which he makes a desperate attempt to break from his bonds and escape. It is said that as often as not he makes it the first time, perhaps at the expense of one or two legs, but seldom does he escape from a second female.

In another araneid, *Meta segmentata* from Europe, both sexes are of similar proportions, though the male is longer-legged and slimmer-bodied than the female. Here you would expect the male to be in little danger, but despite his relatively large size he still takes some precautions, only mating with the female when she is engaged in feeding on an insect that she has lately caught and wrapped in silk.

Size seems to influence the chances of survival of males of the European garden or cross spider, *Araneus diadematus*, a species introduced by man into North America. Courtship in this species is fraught with danger for the male, for if he is not very careful in his approach to the female, he is likely to end up being eaten. It would seem that smaller males come off worst, for females of any size are more likely to make a meal of such males. One interesting and surprising aspect of cannibalism is that females who have eaten a male gain more weight and produce larger egg batches. As long as he has mated beforehand, therefore, a cannibalized male will at least have guaranteed greater biological success by increasing the number of his offspring.

If we look more closely at this species, we find that evolution has made the task of the male garden spider difficult enough as it is, for all the chips seem to be stacked against him in his attempts to achieve his goal of mating successfully with the female of his choice. In the first place, she is much bigger than him and tends to be rather ferocious.

Second, the male spider has to persuade the female to step onto a special thread that he has produced before he will mate with her. If he has achieved his aim once, without being eaten, he then has to repeat the whole dangerous process, for in this spider the male only discharges one palp at a time, and he therefore breaks off the engagement before attempting to mate for the second time.

In at least one other araneid, *Araneus quadratus*, the male has found a way of sometimes overcoming the problems associated with a larger, vicious female.

If he is lucky, he will find an immature female and stay with her in her lair until she undergoes her final molt to become adult and mature. Then, as soon as she has completed this molt, and while her jaws have not yet hardened, he mates with her. Failing this, the *A. quadratus* male has to undergo a trial of terror similar to that of the garden spider. The same ploy is used by males of the fierce gnaphosid hunting spider genus *Drassodes*.

COUNTERMEASURES

In a number of spiders, the male has evolved a method of locking the female's jaws while mating is taking place, thus reducing the danger he is in, at least until it is time to let go and retreat. This is not uncommon in the mygalomorphs, where courtship proceeds in a face-to-face fashion until the female is tempted into the threat attitude in which the jaws are opened wide. At this point, the male then locks her jaws open by means

GOOD-HUMORED MATING

Zygiella xnotata is found around human habitation on both sides of the North Atlantic. Courtship in this species seems to be very good-humored, with the male first tempting the female out of her lair by plucking on the line that runs between the latter and the web center. When eventually the female responds by leaving the lair, she in turn signals to the male by plucking at the web. There is then a brief period of flirtation during which they play a kind of "pat-a-cake" with each other's legs before the male is allowed to mate.

Male grass spiders of the genus Tetragnatha *from Europe and North America use their jaws to lock open those of their mates during mating. The interlocking pegs on the male's (lower) and female's (upper) jaws can clearly be seen (left). Once their jaws are locked, mating can proceed (opposite). The slightly slimmer-bodied male has introduced his inflated palpal organ into the female epigyne, and sperm is being pumped into the female's spermathecae.*

56

of special spiny spurs situated on the front legs.

This is not, however, necessarily the case with the big-jawed, grass or stilt spiders of the family *Tetragnathidae*. *Tetragnatha* males enter the female's web and advance toward her with jaws agape. She then advances to meet him with her jaws wide open also. Careful co-ordination means that, as they meet, their front legs come into contact, and the male is then able to push her legs out sideways and at the same time he shoves his jaws between hers. On his jaws are special spurs which lock into opposing spurs on her jaws, enabling him to keep them forced wide open. Once she is thus immobilized, he is able to mate with her quite safely. Sadly for *Tetragnatha* males, however, their leap backward to safety after mating is complete is not always successful.

In the North American linyphiid bowl-and-doily spider, males and females undertake a false or pseudocopulation during which no sperm is transferred, and the male is able to assess by means of some signal from the female, whether or not she is a virgin. If she is, the male then constructs his sperm web, charges his palps and mates with her. In the laboratory, however, it was discovered that if the female is not a virgin, the male then never builds a sperm web. This system seems to have evolved to prevent the male from wasting precious resources, in the form of sperm, upon a previously mated female.

SPIDER GUARDS

Another linyphiid, the sierra dome spider, *Linyphia litigiosa*, lives in forested valleys throughout the mountains of western North America. Mature males actively seek immature females and on finding one they guard her, often for a number of days, until she matures. Once the female has undergone her final molt to maturity, they then mate immediately. Very immature females or those which have already mated may also be guarded, but never for more than a day. A male who is guarding a female will defend his position vigorously against other males who wish to usurp him. These fights may eventually end up with the death of one of the participants so that in the end it is the fittest male who mates with the female.

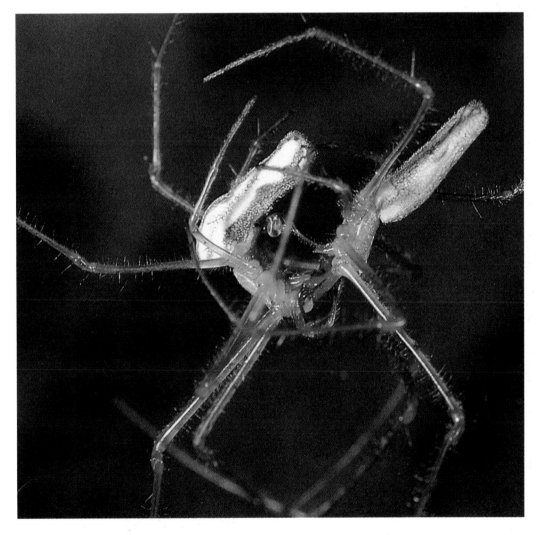

MATING

Following the often complicated courtship ritual, the mating process in spiders is relatively straightforward, despite the complexities of structure in the male palp and the female epigyne of many of the true spiders. Whatever the courtship procedure, mating males normally attain one of two positions. They either face the female and, tipping her gently backward, insert the palps into the epigyne, or alternatively they sit on her back and reach over her abdomen sideways to achieve the same end. The latter position has its advantages in that the male is, in many instances, able to sit over the female's cephalothorax, keeping her jaws well out of reach. Where the male is tiny compared to the female, he just has to hang beneath her while he mates. Mygalomorph males, with their simple palps, often place both together into the epigyne, but in true spiders one palp at a time is usually used.

Exceptions to this rule occur in males of the true spider families *Pholcidae, Oonopidae, Dysderidae* and *Scytodidae*, who insert both palps simultaneously. These families are in fact quite primitive, and the method of mating in the *Pholcidae* and the *Scytodidae* retains some of the most ancient of spider characteristics, for the inserting of the sperm into the female takes place using both the palps and the jaws. Although it is not clear by what mechanism the palpal organ fills with semen, it is known that it is emptied by increasing the blood pressure within the palps so that pressure is exerted on the sperm reservoir, forcing the semen out through the embolus. During mating, some male spiders withdraw the palp at intervals and chew it, which evidently plays some role in the emptying process.

The relative positions of mating jumping spiders, with the male leaning over the female's abdomen, show up clearly in this pair of Evarcha falcata *(left) from Europe. Mating in the pair of European* Agelena labyrinthica *(above) is taking place at the entrance to the female's lair.*

Having been accepted by the female, male wolf spiders, such as the European Pardosa amentata *(right), climb onto their male's cephalothorax while mating. This allows them to hold the female's jaws out of harm's way while they lean over sideways and introduce their palpal organs, one at a time, into the female epigyne.*

BASIC MATING POSITIONS

1 In mygalomorph and some araneomorph spiders, the male approaches the female from the front. He immobilizes her jaws and then inserts his palpal organ into her epigyne.

2 In many araneomorph spiders, the male lies across the front half of the female's body, which has the effect of holding her jaws out of harm's way while he mates with her.

3 In a number of linyphiid spiders, the males have odd-shaped protuberances on their bodies, which the female grasps in her jaws during mating. This ploy of keeping his mate's jaws occupied seems to reduce the likelihood of the male ending up as a meal.

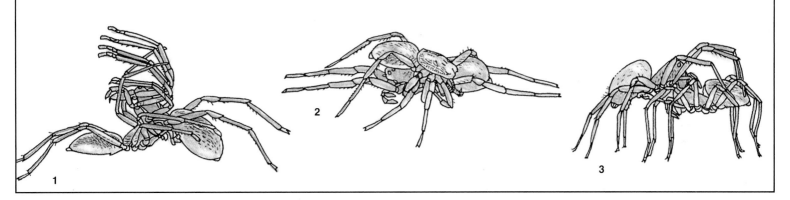

THE LIFE CYCLE

The life cycle of the spider begins with the laying of eggs, whereas scorpions produce live young. Spiders vary in size from around ¹⁄₁₆ in (1 mm) in body length to around 3½ ins (90 mm) and show a proportional variation in the size and number of eggs laid. Once the eggs are laid, their fate depends upon the species concerned; they may just be abandoned, or the female may care for and even feed her offspring after they have hatched. The new-born resemble miniature adults and then grow by means of a series of molts.

Female fisher spiders, Pisaura mirabilis *from Europe, along with closely related American species are good mothers and protect their egg sacs until the young hatch out. In this species, the female holds her egg sac between her jaws and spinnerets, so she is unable to feed again until her offspring emerge.*

EGG-LAYING

Having completed the previous section of the book by considering the mating process, it is convenient to start here with what happens from this point on. The sperm that has been implanted in the female's storage organs, the spermathecae, by the male may remain there unused for a considerable time, during which the eggs develop in the ovaries. When the female is ready to lay her eggs, she first weaves a silken sheet upon which to deposit them, the amount of silk used and the thickness of the sheet varying from family to family. The primitive daddy-long-legs spider *Pholcus*, for example, uses only a few loose threads, while the more advanced spiders of the pisaurid genus *Dolomedes* produce a cup of thickly woven silk into which to deposit their eggs.

As the spider lays her eggs onto the silken sheet, she covers them in a sticky liquid that includes the contents of the spermathecae, the sperm from the male. The surface of the egg at this time is very soft and the sperms have no problem in entering and fertilizing it. When observers saw the female lay her eggs without mating taking place shortly beforehand, it was thought that parthenogenesis, that is, the production of offspring from unfertilized eggs, was common in spiders. It is now realized, of course, that this was because of the often long delay between mating and egg-laying. Parthenogenesis is, however, known to occur in some minute tropical spiders from Africa and the West Indies.

The number of eggs laid by the female spider seems to correlate well with her size, in that tiny spiders lay only a few eggs at a time while larger ones lay many more. There are, however, some species of large spiders that are known to lay just a few very large eggs, the advantage of this being that the larger spiderlings that hatch from them have a better start in life. Females of the giant bird-eating spiders, whose legs can span a dinner plate, may lay up to 3000 eggs at a time, while some of the larger orb-web spiders may lay almost as many.

Not all of the eggs necessarily end up in one egg sac. Sometimes the female will divide them between a number of egg sacs, though the number of eggs in each sac gradually falls off with time. At the other end of the scale, females of tiny spiders such as *Oonops domesticus*, a common European indoor species less than 0.08 in (2 mm) long, are known to lay only two eggs at a time, while a minute cave spider is reported to produce a single egg. As you would expect, the size of these eggs is also variable, with the bigger species laying the bigger eggs. The range of sizes known in spider eggs lies between roughly 0.02 in (4 mm) for the smallest and roughly 0.2 in (4 mm) in some of the large mygalomorphs.

Theridion sisyphium (left) from Europe hangs her grayish-green egg sac in her lair and protects it until the young hatch. Around her can be seen the remains of various prey items, including what looks very much like the body of her erstwhile mate.

The beautifully marked female wolf spider (top right) belongs to the genus Hippasa and comes from Kenya. She is demonstrating the typical method, employed by free-living members of her kind, of carrying her egg sac attached to her spinnerets, leaving her jaws free to catch her prey.

Araniella cucurbitina (right), who is found on both sides of the Atlantic, swathes her egg sac in copious amounts of straw-colored silk, making it more difficult for parasitic wasps to lay their eggs on the spider's eggs inside.

PROTECTING THE EGGS

Having completed the laying of her eggs, the female now envelopes them in more silk, the amount again varying from family to family. *Pholcus* uses just a few threads and carries her loosely tied egg-mass in her jaws, while many females lay down a series of layers of silk to produce a protective cocoon for the eggs. *Dolomedes*, for example, continues production of her egg sac by drawing ribbons of silk across the mass of eggs in the previously formed silk cup until everything is swathed in silk. She holds the egg sac in her front three pairs of legs and, hanging from her silken bridge by her fourth pair of legs, rotates it. As she does so, she presses it with her palps, legs and abdomen so that it forms a near sphere, at the same time coating it with further layers of silk. In general, spiders who remain with their eggs until they hatch or alternatively hide them well away in a burrow, under a stone or rolled up in a leaf, tend to use less silk to cover them than those who abandon their eggs once the egg sac is finished.

The fate of the completed egg sac depends upon the type of spider that has produced it. Burrowing spiders, as you might expect, leave their egg sacs within the safety of their burrows, and unless you dig them up, you are unlikely to see them. Other spiders lay their eggs beneath stones, logs or under bark, and they may be found by searching for them.

TRANSPORTING THE EGGS

Many of the active hunters carry their egg sacs with them until the young hatch. Females of the *Pisauridae*, such as *Dolomedes*, which has species in the U.S.A., Europe, and Australia, *Pisaurina* from the U.S.A. and *Pisaura* from Europe all guard their egg sacs by holding them attached to their spinnerets.

Pisaurina mira from much of the U.S.A. east of the Rocky Mountains and *Pisaura mirabilis* from Europe are both inhabitants of bushes and low vegetation along woodland and meadow edges, where they may commonly be seen in summer sitting on leaves to expose their egg sacs to the warmth of the sun. Certain of the burrowing members of the *Lycosidae* will come to the entrance of their burrow after a spell of cool weather in order to warm their egg sacs.

Many of the lycosids are, however, wandering hunters, and the female carries her egg sac with her at all times. Unlike the pisaurids, the lycosids hold their egg sacs by the spinnerets only, leaving their jaws free and with the advantage that they can continue to catch prey and feed. Female crab spiders and lynx spiders attach their egg sacs to the undersides of leaves and stones, on the bark of trees or among the foliage of plants, and then sit astride them on guard. Jumping spider females find similar places in which to build a silken retreat which protects both them and their egg sacs. A number of mainly tropical families contain species which are somewhat flattened and spend their lives on the surface of tree trunks. These spiders are usually colored to match lichens and algae which grow on the bark, and they use pieces of these to camouflage their flattened egg sacs.

The behavior of female theridiids is quite variable in that some lay their egg sacs out of sight and sit and protect them, others hang them on threads in their webs, while yet others build a lair in which they lay their eggs and then remain on guard over their egg sacs. The behavior of the *Araneidae* also varies, some spiders keeping their egg sacs with them in the web while others hang them in vegetation close to the web and then abandon them. The American araneid, *Mecynogea lemniscata*, lays several batches of eggs in separate sacs and then collapses her dome-shaped horizontal web around them before wrapping them all in further layers of protective silk. It is clear, therefore, that many spiders are good mothers and protect their developing young while they are in the egg sac, though not all of them will survive long enough to see the spiderlings emerge. How those females that survive this period of guarding their egg sacs treat their young when they emerge will be described later.

DEVELOPMENT OF THE EMBRYO

The embryo spider develops within a series of membranes surrounding the egg using as food the yolk supplied by the female spider. At the time of hatching, the number of these membranes which are broken out of and subsequently discarded varies from family to family and has in the past led to some problems in naming the developmental stages. The latest system devised to overcome these problems requires the embryo to escape from at least one of these membranes, using an egg-tooth at the base of the palps to pierce it, to become a postembryo. At some stage, the postembryo discards the outer body covering, the integument, to become a first instar, which is then able to leave the egg sac. If you find an egg sac from which

The South African Pholcus *(right) is typical of the genus, holding her eggs, loosely tied with a few silken strands, in her jaws.* Peucetia lucasii *(left), a lynx spider from the dry tropical forest of the island of Madagascar, makes a more substantial egg sac characteristic of her genus and stands guard over it.*

The egg sacs of Ero *pirate spiders are usually left at the end of a stalk, but this example of a species from South Africa (left) has been covered in a layer of tiny pebbles. The egg sac of the European* Agroeca *(opposite, bottom), on the other hand, is simply covered in wet mud, which soon hardens to form a protective coat.*

the spiderlings have recently escaped and you examine it with a magnifying glass, you may well be able to see the tiny, empty spider integuments that have been left behind.

The first-instar spiderling is a miniature copy of the adult, although when it emerges from the egg sac it is very pale in color. In contact with the air, however, it slowly assumes its normal coloring, which may or may not initially be identical to that of the adult spider. For a while many newly emerged spiders are able to feed on the remaining egg yolk, but eventually they have to start catching prey and feeding themselves. From then on, the spider goes through further instars until it becomes adult.

LOOKING AFTER THE EGG SACS

Spiders who abandon their egg sacs often take extra steps to protect them from possible predators or parasitic insects. Sometimes the sacs are suspended from a long, thin thread, making it difficult for an egg-feeding insect to get to them. In addition, the sac may be covered in a layer of wet mud, which on hardening provides some extra protection against the ovipositors of parasitic wasps. In addition to mud, pieces of wood, leaf or even tiny stones may be stuck on the outside to camouflage the egg sac from birds and other sharp-sighted vertebrates. The Australian platform spider *Corasoides* leaves her egg sacs in her burrow while the young are developing. She binds a layer of soil debris with silk around the spherical sacs, and when she is finished they are virtually indistinguishable from rabbit pellets.

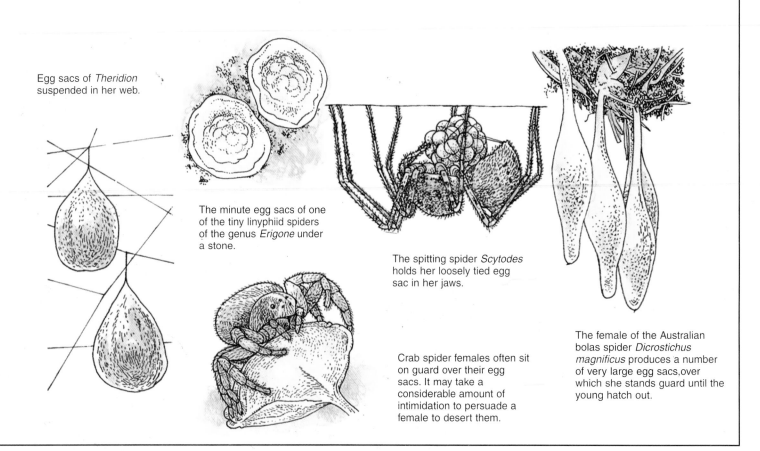

Egg sacs of *Theridion* suspended in her web.

The minute egg sacs of one of the tiny linyphiid spiders of the genus *Erigone* under a stone.

The spitting spider *Scytodes* holds her loosely tied egg sac in her jaws.

Crab spider females often sit on guard over their egg sacs. It may take a considerable amount of intimidation to persuade a female to desert them.

The female of the Australian bolas spider *Dicrostichus magnificus* produces a number of very large egg sacs, over which she stands guard until the young hatch out.

EGG-SAC PRODUCTION

1 The female constructs a platform of silk, on which the eggs are to be laid.

2 She holds her abdomen over the platform and begins to lay her eggs. At the same time, she releases semen, which has been stored in her spermathecae, to fertilize them.

3 Having laid all her eggs, the female now swathes them in further layers of silk to form a strong, protective coat.

4 Having completed her egg sac, the female pisaurid now attaches it to her spinnerets, grabs it in her jaws and continues her daily routine.

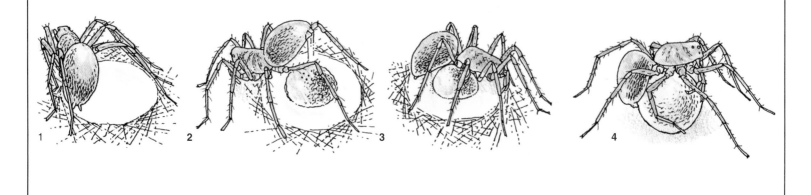

CARE OF THE SPIDERLINGS

The fate of the young spiders once they leave the relative safety of the egg sac varies between spiders and often relates to the way in which the female treated them in the first place. Spiderlings emerging from egg sacs which have been abandoned by the female are clearly on their own from the start. They may remain together in a group for a while, but once they have used up any remaining yolk, they then disperse and lead independent lives. Where hundreds of spiderlings emerge from the same sac and disperse, there may be some cannibalism among them if supplies of food happen to be short at the time.

BURROWING SPIDERS

Many burrowing spiders keep their egg sacs within the burrows, and in many of these the young may stay with their mother for a considerable time before they disperse to lead independent lives. Development from egg to adult in the European mygalomorph trapdoor spider, *Nemesia caementaria*, for example, takes anything from three to five years, for two or three of which the young remain in the female's burrow feeding upon prey captured by her.

CARRYING THE SPIDERLINGS

Both in Europe and the U.S.A., there are many species of the lycosid genus *Pardosa*. They occupy a range of different habitats, but are basically small, seldom exceeding 0.4 in (10 mm) in length. They are ground-living spiders dressed in somber hues of brown and black, though they may have patches of white bristles on the front legs and palps. They are spiders of late spring and summer, when they may be seen running around in suburban gardens in search of prey. The female is very noticeable when she is carrying her egg sac behind her on her spinnerets, and she may often be seen sitting in a patch of sunlight keeping her eggs warm to encourage their development. Continued watching of her antics over a period of days will reveal a sudden change in her appearance, for one day you will see her with her egg sac intact; the next it will have gone and instead she will appear to have grown a fur coat. In the interim, she will have cut open her egg sac for the spiderlings to emerge, for unlike spiderlings of many other species, they are unable to do this themselves. These newly

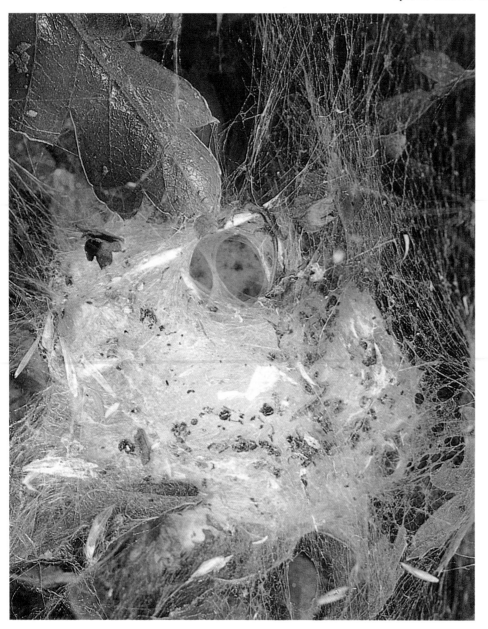

PROVIDING A NURSERY

We have already seen how the spiders *Pisaura mirabilis* from Europe and *Pisaurina mira* from the U.S.A. carry their egg sacs around with them. They also do not desert their young immediately they hatch. Instead they build a silk nursery tent in which they place the newly hatched spiderlings. Here they remain, with the female on guard, until they have undergone their second molt, when they disperse. This particular pattern of parental care has earned these species the common name of nursery-tent spiders.

hatched offspring then immediately climb upon her back to form her "fur coat." There they remain for several days without feeding, but they then undergo their second molt and disperse.

Coelotes terrestris is a European agelenid which lives in a burrow that it excavates beneath a stone or log. It lines this burrow with silk and builds a silken collar at the entrance. The female rushes out of the burrow to catch insects that walk past its entrance and these she shares with her offspring, which live with her. They spend between four and eight weeks in the company of their mother, and as they grow she catches more and more prey for them. Research carried out on this spider has revealed that when the spiderlings are small and their food requirements are at a minimum, the female spends a lot of time manipulating and feeding on the prey herself. As they grow, they actively stimulate her to spend more time catching food for them. She does not live for long once winter sets in, though her offspring continue to occupy her burrow until spring comes, when they disperse. There is some evidence that the young of this species feed on their dead mother's corpse.

SIBLING BEHAVIOR

In the North American lycosid spider, *Geolycosa turricola*, which lives in burrows in the ground, research has shown that sibling spiderlings (brothers and sisters) show a high degree of tolerance to one another, rather than the cannibalism that can occur in other spiders. It is believed that this behavior, by letting them feed upon prey captured by their mother, allows them to disperse eventually at a larger size, thus increasing their chances of survival. This degree of tolerance of one another must also be present in those nonburrowing species where the young remain with the female.

The female European labyrinth spider Agelina labyrinthica *(left), as her name implies, builds a complex labyrinth of silk in the center of her sheet web in which she lays her eggs and then stands on guard over them. It is believed that this makes it difficult for egg predators and parasites to find the eggs. The garden spider* Araneus diadematus, *however, leaves her egg sac unattended, so that the newly hatched spiderlings (right) are afforded no protection by their mother. They remain in a ball like this for several days and then disperse.*

Females of actively hunting wolf spiders, such as those of the genus Pardosa *from Europe and the U.S.A., carry their young on their backs for the first few days of their lives; the example (inset) is of* P. nigriceps *from Europe. The closely related pisaurid spiders include the large* Dolomedes *species, which is also found on both sides of the Atlantic The* Dolomedes *spiderlings recently emerged from an egg sac give an idea of the reproductive capacity of some species of spiders (left).*

The ultimate in parental care in spiders occurs in some members of the family Theridiidae. Theridion sisyphium *(opposite) from Europe is the best documented of these, for the female actually feeds her young from her mouth (see box below). There are, however, some recent reports that members of the related genus* Achaearanea, *such as the species (below left) from the rainforests of Panama, also protect and feed their young.*

SPIDERS' MILK

The most advanced form of parental care in spiders is found in certain members of the family *Theridiidae*; the best documented of these is the European species, *Theridion sisyphium*. The female of this spider places her egg sac in a silken tent which forms her lair. Newly hatched young are fed upon liquid which she regurgitates from her mouth, a sort of "spiders' milk." As they grow, they share the food which she has caught, though initially she breaks it up for them with her stronger jaws. As a result, the prey's liquefying body contents can escape for the young to suck up. They eventually reach a size where they can assist their mother in capturing prey.

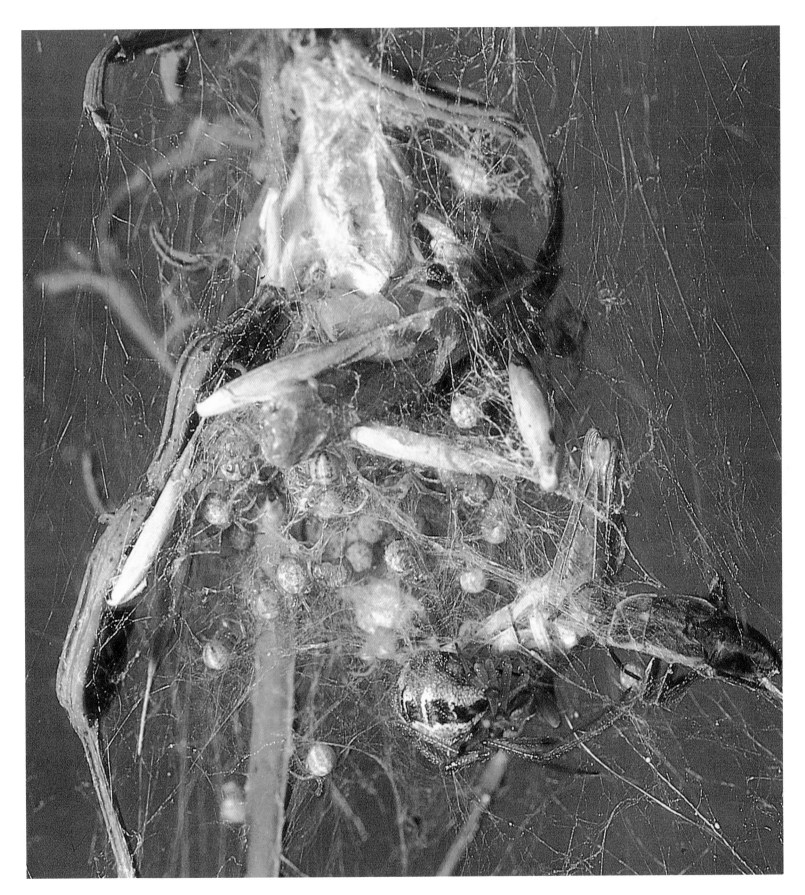

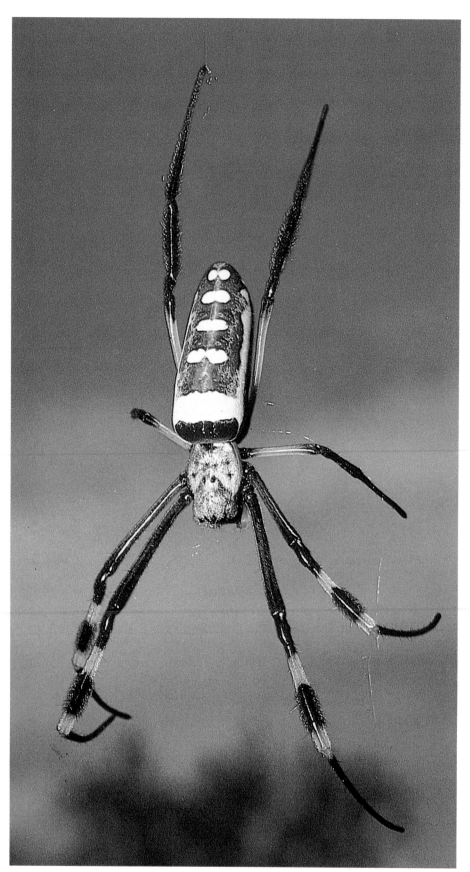

MOLTING AND REGENERATION

Like all other arthropods, spiders grow by feeding and at regular intervals shedding their old exoskeleton and replacing it with another, a phenomenon we refer to as molting, or ecdysis. The mechanism involved in all arachnids is very much the same and therefore a description of how the process takes place in spiders will also cover the other groups. The only real differences are likely to be where molting takes place rather than how.

THE EXOSKELETON

Before considering the molting process itself, let's take a quick look at how the exoskeleton is made up. The body is covered in a series of plates, and the appendages are formed from tubes, all of them to a greater or lesser extent unable to stretch. Between these are softer, flexible interconnecting membranes which permit relative movement between the different parts of the body. Since the exoskeleton cannot stretch, it has to be replaced by a new one from beneath. In order for this to stretch to the spider's new size and then harden off it has to be produced in a slightly folded state.

During the period before molting takes place, the spider builds up the materials necessary for the production of the new exoskeleton. Not all of the materials in the old exoskeleton are lost when molting takes place, for they have an intrinsic value to the spider. Instead, as much as can be is digested and reabsorbed back into the spider's body for further use. Despite this, there is still some loss of energy over the whole series of molts up to adulthood. Recent researches have shown that in some spiders as much as 20 percent of postembryonic growth production is lost during molting, though figures as low as 5.2 percent have been recorded. The greatest loss of energy occurs in large female mygalomorphs, who molt at intervals throughout their often long life and may as a result lose as much as 50 percent of their growth production.

Nephila senegalensis *(left) from Africa is a member of a genus of orb-web spiders that is widespread in the tropical and subtropical regions of the world. Her beautiful and distinctive pattern would not have been complete until she underwent her final molt into adulthood.*

THE MOLTING PROCESS

The molting process is known to be under the control of the same hormone as that found in other arthropods, namely ecdysone. Since during ecdysis the old exoskeleton is gradually broken down, there has to be a period beforehand when the spider ceases to feed. The position adopted by the spider during molting depends rather upon whether it is a mygalomorph or a true spider, and whether it is free-living or a burrowing species. The spider is very vulnerable both to attack over the period prior to and during molting and to drying out during the latter, so it has to afford itself at least some kind of protection. For the spiders which live in burrows, this is no real problem, but for the rest there are two choices. Those spiders which are vagrant hunters and therefore have no permanent residence often construct a special silken retreat in which to molt. For obvious reasons, this is usually well hidden. Alternatively they may retreat to some nook or cranny where they hang head down from a single silken strand. Spiders which are resident in a permanent web also hang from a single silken line and molt in this position.

Whatever position spiders adopt in order to carry out their molt, the actual mechanisms involved are identical. In the hours leading up to the molt, when the final separation of the old cuticle from the new one beneath it is taking place, the spider appears to all intents and purposes dead. The first sign that something is indeed going on is when the old cuticle begins to split from the head end backward along the sides of the carapace just above the level of the legs. This split then continues backward along the waist and down both sides of the abdomen. From this moment on, the

THE NUMBER OF MOLTS

The number of times a spider molts varies somewhat, but normally larger species undergo a greater number than smaller species; and males, because they are often smaller than females, tend to molt fewer times. Whereas the true spiders do not molt again once they have reached adulthood, the mygalomorphs molt, usually once a year, for the rest of their often long lives. This gives them the ability to replace damaged and wornout surface structures which, if they were not replaced, would place them at a disadvantage. A number of these spiders, for example, carry on the abdominal surface a carpet of hairs which serve a defensive purpose. A year after its previous molt, such a spider might have a nearly naked abdomen and therefore lack an important means of defense which can only be replaced by a further molt.

THE MOLTING PROCESS

1 A split appears along the side of the carapace above the level of the legs.

2 The split continues along the side of the abdomen, and the spider begins to emerge from the old skin, starting at the head end.

3 Once the body is free, the spider begins to withdraw its appendages from the old cuticle, starting with the jaws.

4 With its whole body now free of the old skin, the spider begins to stretch the new one to its full size.

5 The spider now hangs for a while, flexing its legs and palps, while the new skin dries off and hardens.

spider begins actively to withdraw its appendages from the confines of the old cuticle. First the jaws are extracted, followed by the palps and then one by one the pairs of legs are pulled out, starting with the front pair and working backward. Once the legs are free, the spider is then able to extract itself easily from the old abdominal cuticle.

The new cuticle is wrinkled, and is still moist and pliable from the molting fluid that has been secreted between it and the old exoskeleton. The spider now has to use the pressure of the fluid in its body cavity to stretch the new exoskeleton before it dries out. At this stage the spider may be seen to flex and bend its legs and palps and work its jaws in order to maintain the flexibility of its joints, for it has been found that if a leg is, for some reason, unable to move at this time, then it remains stiff and inflexible. On the occasions when this does occur, the spider may itself eventually bite the useless leg off.

A close examination of the newly emerged spider reveals that not only has the old exoskeleton been replaced in its entirety, but so also have all the tactile hairs, trichobothria and other structures which abound on its surface. The linings of the foregut and hindgut have also been replaced, for these are made up of an impermeable layer of cuticle. The newly emerged spider is at first very pale in color, much like the newly hatched spiderling, but as the skin comes into contact with the air and dries and hardens, it begins to take on its normal coloring. Molting is a very traumatic event for all spiders, and a percentage of them die during the process.

REGENERATION

Spiders and other arachnids, in common with many other arthropods, are able to replace appendages which have been lost or damaged, though how successful this regeneration is depends upon the stage of development that the animal has reached. In general, the earlier the stage at which regeneration begins, the more likely it will be completed before the final molt to adulthood, for at this point such a regrowth is no longer possible, with one exception. This exception again occurs in the mygalomorphs, for they are able to regenerate lost appendages gradually with each succeeding molt during their prolonged adult phase.

AUTOTOMY

The appendage that requires regeneration may be one that the spider has shed on purpose as a means of escaping from a predator which has grabbed hold of it. This phenomenon, known as autotomy, means the appendage can break off at a predetermined weak point. In spiders this is between the coxa and trochanter, but in other arachnids it may be elsewhere. In harvestmen, for example, the break occurs between the trochanter and the femur. The importance of breaking at this weak point rather than at some other position is that at the weak point there is a system for shutting off the blood circulation so that the spider does not die of a hemorrhage. Since a fatal hemorrhage is inevitable in the eventuality of a break elsewhere, the spider itself will endeavor to cut the limb off at the weak point. In order, apparently, not to waste its vital body fluids, the spider will pick up an autotomized appendage and suck the blood out of it, a process called autophagy, before it discards it completely.

An unusual instance of self-autotomy is found in the diminutive males of the American theridiid genus *Tidarren*. These males, as adults, only have a single, enormous palp, which they carry held out in front of them. Were they to possess two of these monstrous appendages in adulthood, it is highly unlikely that they would be able to use either of them, so two stages before its molt to maturity, the male twists one of them off. It is very interesting that, unlike the case with appendages that have broken off accidentally, the *Tidarren* palps never show any sign of regrowth.

Since spiders usually molt in some hidden corner, it is not very often that an observer is lucky enough to see the process in action. This Pisaura mirabilis *female (opposite) completed her molt some time ago, for she has already assumed her full coloration. A careful examination of the picture shows that she is still attached to a length of silk from her spinnerets. The old cuticle is still present, the tarsal claws clinging to the grass stem from which she hung before she began her molt.*

DISPERSAL AND LONGEVITY

Since the number of spiderlings that emerge from a single egg sac is generally far in excess of the number of adult spiders that could successfully occupy the immediate environment, the young have to disperse to pastures new. As with most things to do with spiders, the degree to which the young disperse away from their place of birth varies from one species to another. In many of the mygalomorph trapdoor spiders, the young leave their mother's burrow and make one of their own at the nearest convenient point, so that colonies of these creatures may often be found. Otherwise the young move a lesser or greater distance under their own steam and set up home or adopt a hunting territory as soon as they find somewhere suitable.

BALLOONING

A great number of spider families, however, indulge in a much more interesting form of dispersal, namely that of ballooning. Ballooning is a form of aerial dispersal where the spider actually uses a length of silk in place of a balloon, but the principles are the same. Aerial dispersal is common among subadult spiders of many families and is common in adults of many of the *Linyphiidae*, especially within the subfamily *Erigoninae* (which in Britain are known as money spiders). Adults of other families balloon as long as they are small enough. Size precludes flight in even the young of most of the mygalomorphs, but some are light enough to indulge in it.

Whatever their group, ballooning involves the spiders in some sort of maneuver which guarantees that the silk is pulled out of the spinnerets. The best conditions are those when it is warm, with rising air currents and a light wind. If such conditions prevail, the spider may climb to some high point, such as the tip of a grass stem, the end of a twig or the top of a fence post, and face into the breeze. It then lifts the tip of its abdomen high into the air and releases a stream of silk from its spinnerets, though quite how this happens we are not sure, for silk needs a pull on it as it is produced in order for it to set. Once it feels enough pull on the silk to lift it into

DISPERSAL BY BALLOONING

1 The few mygalomorph spiders whose young disperse in this way have been seen to hang down from a piece of thread, which they gradually spin longer and longer until it begins to billow in the wind. At this point, it breaks free at an apparent weak spot near the anchorage point. The spider, attached to its silken parachute, is blown away by the wind.

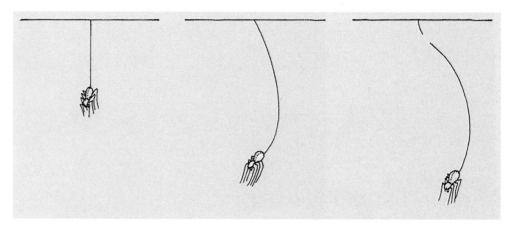

2 In order to effect their dispersal, some araneomorph spiderlings suspend themselves from a long line and then produce a loop of silk, which is gradually drawn away from the spinnerets by the breeze. Once the spiderling feels that there is sufficient pull on the loop, it cuts itself free of the vertical line and balloons away up into the air.

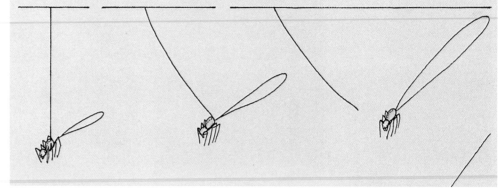

3 The most commonly seen method of dispersal in araneomorphs, both adults and spiderlings, involves an initial climb to some high point, where the animal faces into the wind and raises its abdomen. A length of silk is then released into the breeze until there is sufficient pull on it, at which point the spider lets go and is lifted up into the air.

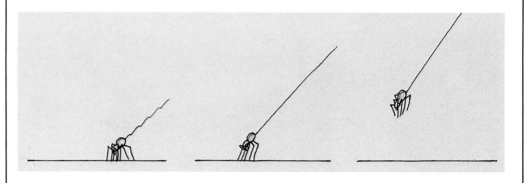

the air, the spider lets go and floats gently away. Alternatively, the spider may hang down on a short thread and then attach another thread to this line, which it then pulls out to form a short loop. As the breeze catches the loop, the spider releases more silk, which is then pulled out until enough is released for the spider to fly. Then it cuts loose from the hanging thread, and off it goes. Ballooning mygalomorphs lower themselves down from a suitable high spot until enough silk has been released for the weight of the spider to break it near its original point of attachment. This causes the spider to drop, but as it does so, the breeze catches the silk and draws the spiderling up and away into the air.

Most spiders probably only travel short distances by ballooning, so that they remain in the same general locality in an environment to which

they are suited. Sometimes, however, they may get lifted by thermals up to great heights where they may be dispersed over very long distances. These unfortunates are seldom likely to survive, for the likelihood of their landing in a suitable habitat so far from their original home is very remote.

LONGEVITY

Once the young spiders have dispersed and established themselves in their new home, how long do they live? Most true spiders in temperate regions live for roughly one year; that is, from the moment the eggs hatch in one season to the time that they lay their eggs in the next, for the female often dies after she has completed laying.

Males may live an even shorter time, dying once they have mated; females who look after their egg sac and/or care for their young survive for some weeks longer. Tropical species may live a little longer, since they do not have to face the problems of overwintering, and the same is true of species which occupy our homes, where they are protected from climatic extremes.

THE LONGEST-LIVED SPIDERS

The longest-lived of the spiders are to be found among the mygalomorphs. In the European trapdoor spider, *Nemesia caementaria*, for example, the female does not become adult until the thirteenth molt, and she may live for as long as 20 years. The males, on becoming adult, cease feeding, and they eventually die from mating exhaustion or are eaten.

Only a small proportion of adult spiders are able to survive the rigors of winter in the temperate regions of the world. It seems a shame that this attractive little female jumping spider Marpissa muscosa *(below left), photographed during an English summer, has but a few short months to live.*
The longest-lived of all spiders are mygalomorph females, such

WOODLAND SPIDERS

Northern, temperate, deciduous woodland of the kind that may be found in the U.S.A. or Europe. Beneath the canopy formed by the dominant tree species is a layer of shrubs and herbs. The woodland floor is covered in a layer of rotting fallen leaves. In this kind of habitat, numerous spider species exist, occupying their own particular ecological niches from the tops of the highest trees down into the leaf litter itself. Flowers such as the foxglove often provide a suitable refuge for the ambushing crab spiders such as *Xysticus* **(1)**, which here has managed to catch a fly investigating the flower. Wherever there is room between adjacent plants, you are likely to find the delicate constructions of one or more species of orb-web spider. Like the *Xysticus*, the large female garden spider *Araneus diadematus* **(2)**, sitting at the center of her web, has recently caught a flying insect which she has wrapped in silk and which is suspended in the web below her. Sitting on a log and taking advantage of the warm sun filtering through gaps in the canopy is a female *Pardosa* wolf spider **(3)** with her egg sac attached to her spinnerets. Lurking in the gloom of the woodland floor at the entrance to her tubular lair is a female *Coelotes terrestris* **(4)**, while waiting on a grass leaf to ambush her prey is the attractive green sparassid *Micrommata virescens* **(5)**.

Scale

1 *Xysticus*,
³⁄₁₆ in (7 mm).

2 *Araneus diadematus*,
⅞ in (40 mm).

3 *Pardosa* wolf spider,
³⁄₁₆ in (7 mm).

4 *Coelotes terrestris*,
⁷⁄₁₆ in (11 mm).

5 *Micrommata virescens*,
⁹⁄₁₆ in (14 mm).

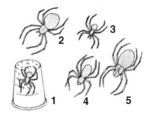

PREY CAPTURE

Spiders employ some of the most ingenious methods of prey capture in the animal kingdom. A large number of species hunt their prey by randomly searching and then pouncing. The alternatives are to lie in wait or to be an ambusher like the crab spiders. Spider prey capture is associated by most people with the spider web. A large number of different types of web have evolved, from the extremely complex – orb- or scaffold-webs – to the ridiculous – a single, sticky strand of silk. A number of species combine individual webs into social groups where captured prey is shared.

More bizarre methods are used by some species; to find out more about angling spiders, spiders that throw nets over their prey, and spiders that spit gum at their prey, read on.

Although vertebrates are not major prey items, spiders will take them if they get the opportunity. The wandering spider Cupiennius coccineus *from Costa Rica has here taken one of the tiny tree frogs that abound in the tropical rainforests of the area.*

THE AMBUSH

The word ambush means "to lie in wait for," which is what a large number of spiders do in order to catch their prey. To the spider there are both advantages and disadvantages to this method of prey capture. The great advantage is that relatively little energy is expended in searching for and chasing prey, and the energy saved can be channeled into more important activities such as the production of eggs or sperm. The great disadvantage is that the spider has to depend upon prey items actually coming within reach, and these may be few and far between. Although certain spider families, for example the crab spiders, are always thought of as being the archetypal ambushing spiders, such tactics may be found in a number of others.

Strictly speaking, all of the mygalomorph spiders are ambushing spiders, for most of them live in burrows or silken tubes and wait for prey to come to them. Only a few are wandering hunters, capturing whatever manageable prey they come into contact with during their travels. The basic technique of the subterranean mygalomorphs is to lie in wait at the entrance to their burrow and then jump out on any suitable prey which happens to walk past. They are aided by the sensitive body hairs which pick up soil-borne vibrations from the approaching prey. Some have, however, improved their chances of success by, as it were, being able to cast their nets a little wider.

DIGGING A BURROW

Before they can catch any prey, they have of course to dig their burrows, often in quite hard soil, and they are well adapted to carry out this labor. Digging is done with the powerful jaws, which have on their margins a comb of large spines to facilitate the process. Particles of earth cut from the walls of the burrow are molded into balls, carried outside and then discarded. The walls of the burrow are then waterproofed with a smooth coat of a mixture of soil and saliva, and all or part of it is lined with silk. Although the occupant cannot turn around throughout most of its length, there is usually a section of the burrow in which this is possible. The diameter and length of the burrow are enlarged as the spider grows, and it is rare for it to be deserted voluntarily by its occupant. Not all mygalomorphs are so hard-working, however, for some of them just construct a simple silk-lined burrow under a log or rock with the minimum of digging.

TRAP-DOOR AMBUSHERS

Most mygalomorph spiders dig burrows, often with a trap door covering the entrance, in which they spend much of their lives. Here they lie in wait, picking up the tiny vibrations transmitted through the earth by prey walking on the surface.

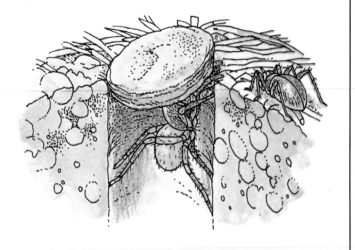

As soon as the spider detects that her prey is within striking distance, she shoots out of the burrow and pounces on it. Her large fangs soon dispatch the unfortunate victim, and it is then dragged into the burrow to be consumed at the spider's leisure.

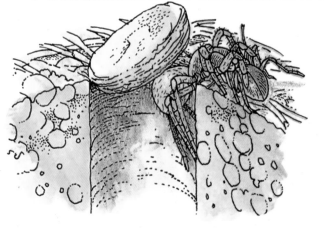

Not all so-called trap-door spiders actually construct a trap door. Some, like the Lyrognathus *female (opposite) from Malaysia, lie in ambush just inside the entrance to their unlidded burrow, from where they leap upon any passing prey.*

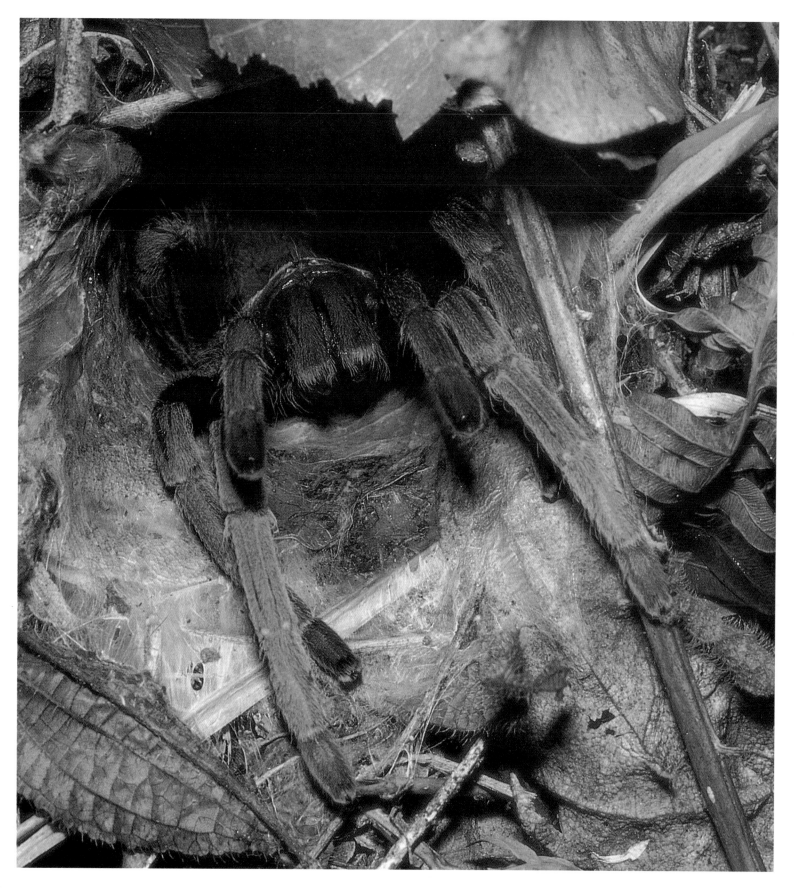

LAYING THE TRAP

Many mygalomorphs have a simple trap door at the entrance to their burrow beneath which they sit in wait, sometimes with the front pair of legs just sticking out from beneath the trap door. They then rush out and grab any suitable prey which comes within reach. This system has been improved upon by a number of species who, by using tripwires, are able to detect prey at a greater distance from the burrow entrance, thus increasing their area of capture. In their simplest form, these tripwires just consist of a number of threads radiating like the spokes of a wheel from the burrow entrance. The spider lies in wait at the burrow entrance with its legs spread out across the triplines, and any scurrying arthropod which is unfortunate enough to stumble across one of them is immediately pounced upon and dragged into the dark depths of the spider's subterranean lair. Interestingly, a similar setup is used by some true spiders, except that they use natural holes and crevices rather than digging their own burrows.

Spiders of the family *Segestriidae* have a tubular body to fit into the holes in which they dwell. They line these with silk and from the mouth of the tube radiate their tripwires, which function in the same manner as those of the trap-door spiders. The Australian twig-line spider has gone one better than this, for it does not even have to use precious silk in constructing its tripwires. Instead it uses twin twigs, leaf stalks and other such debris to form a series of spokes radiating from the burrow entrance and uses them in the same way as the silk tripwires described above.

THE ULTIMATE AMBUSH

The archetypal ambushing spiders are undoubtedly the members of the true spider family, the *Thomisidae* or crab spiders. They deserve their common name from their typical broad, squat carapace and abdomen and their scuttling habits, which are reminiscent of those of a crab. They typically sit with the two powerful front pairs of legs held out ready to grasp any insect that comes too close in a deadly embrace. If the spider is in luck and an insect is caught, it is very rapidly dispatched with the spider's venomous bite. Their ability to kill insects several times their own size is testimony to the effectiveness of their venom. They are very short-sighted and count upon their immobility to prevent them from being detected by approaching prey. Since many species sit openly upon plants to await the arrival of prey, they are often well camouflaged, and this, combined with their immobility, hides them from the sharp eyes of their vertebrate predators.

The crab spider *Misumena vatia* is found on both sides of the Atlantic Ocean, and its favored ambushing sites are white or yellow flowers. Here they sit in wait for their prey – bees, hoverflies, butterflies and other insects that visit the flowers to collect pollen and nectar. What makes them choose one particular flower or flowerhead on which to sit rather than another? The probable answer has come from some recent interesting research carried out in the U.S.A.

In Maine, this spider often sits in wait for prey on the umbels of the milkweed plant *Asclepias syriaca*. If potential prey insects were prevented from visiting a group of these plants, the spiders on those plants did not move to a better-quality flowerhead, i.e., they did not move from few-flowered umbels to many-flowered umbels that would presumably attract more insects. However, when the insects were allowed to visit the plants, the spiders tended to move onto the umbels which had the most flowers

THE PURSE-WEB SPIDERS

One family of mygalomorphs, the *Atypidae* or purse-web spiders, with both American and European representatives, have evolved a unique method of prey capture. Like the trap-door spiders, the females dig a burrow with their specialized jaws and line it with silk, but here the similarity ends. Rather than building a trap door, these spiders extend the silk burrow lining above the soil surface to form a tube. This sealed tube or purse either lies across the ground or may be continued up the trunk of an adjacent tree. In order to camouflage it, they cover the silk with soil and other suitable debris. The spider lies in wait within the silk tube, which is in fact a deadly trap. Should an insect or other arthropod stumble across it, she rushes to that point and thrusts her sharp fangs out through the silk purse wall into the soft underbelly of the luckless victim. She then employs a row of teeth on the basal segment of each jaw to cut through the silk, whereupon she drags the prey into the tube. Having dispatched it, she then returns to repair the hole in the purse before she retires underground to her feast.

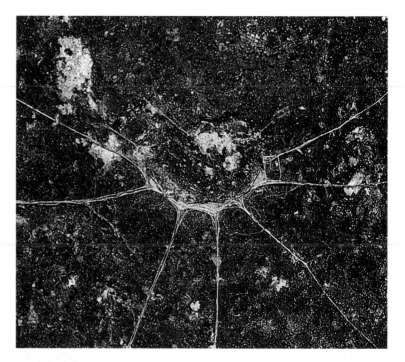

Although the spiders themselves are seldom seen since they remain in their burrows when disturbed, it is hard not to see the system of triplines around the burrow entrance of one of the most primitive of spiders,

Liphistius desultor *(below) from Malaysia. When prey triggers the triplines, the spider emerges and pounces.*

Female purse-web spiders spend all of their lives hidden in their silken tubes, part of which is below and the rest above ground. In order to photograph this European Atypus affinis *female (left), which is similar in appearance to the American species, she has been trapped in her purse above ground and carefully removed. Upon being released, she quickly found her silken tube and made her way back into it.*

THE PURSE-WEB SPIDER IN ACTION

1 The female purse-web spider lies in wait inside her silk purse, which may lie across the ground as here, or runs from the ground up the trunk of a tree in other species.

2 She pierces her prey from below, through the purse, with her huge fangs, and then drags it under ground to eat it.

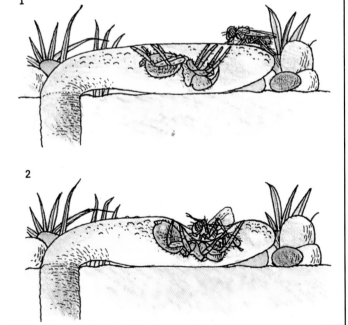

TRAPEZE ARTISTS

If you live in or visit Australia, you might be lucky enough to find a very colorful spider, *Arcys*, apparently made out of wax with a triangular abdomen. This spider sits on leaves and flowers. Its front two pairs of legs are adapted for catching prey, like the typical crab spider, and it ambushes its prey in the same way. What is so unusual about it, however, is that it is not a thomisid crab spider at all, but is an araneid orb-web spider that has almost completely given up the use of a web and has become an ambusher instead. It assumes its crab-spiderlike posture during the hours of daylight, but it also catches prey at night using a web. To describe its web as such is, however, something of a misnomer, for it is a single length of silk strung between two suitable points and from which the spider hangs. These spiders have never been seen catching their prey from this line, but have been found with prey, and it is assumed that they catch insects by grabbing them as they fly past. It is possible they produce a pheromone to attract insects to them.

open. These umbels were the ones which attracted most insects, so it would appear that the spiders are able to respond in some way to the number of insects attracted toward particular umbels and are then stimulated to move to a better position. The stimulus for them to move is somewhat debatable. It may be visual, but they are rather short-sighted; or it could be the vibrations set up by the constant visits of the flying insects.

A female of the crab spider Misumena vatia, *found on both sides of the Atlantic but seen here in England, sits in its favorite ambushing pose (opposite).*

Crab spiders such as this species from New Guinea (below right) are able to take prey as large as the cicada because of their fast-acting venom. Crab spiders are also referred to as flower spiders because of their habit of sitting in ambush on flowers. The Thomisus *from Kenya (below left) is demonstrating the habit admirably.*

THE HUNTERS

Whereas the ambushers lie in wait for their prey and may at the most make a short dash to grab it, the hunters are spiders which actively move around in search of theirs. The hunters come from a number of different families and range from the short-sighted creatures of the night, such as the gnaphosids and clubionids, to those sharp-eyed lovers of the sun, the salticids, oxyopids and lycosids.

NOCTURNAL HUNTERS

The short-sighted nocturnal hunters wander around at night on the ground or on vegetation and catch any prey of suitable size with which they come into contact. To see them you have to turn over stones or look behind peeling bark, where they may often be found passing the daylight hours in a silken retreat; two members of the genus *Herpyllus*, however, may often be found hunting on the walls and ceilings of human habitations at night. In the U.S.A., this will be *H. ecclesiasticus*, the parson spider, which is blackish in color with white abdominal markings, about 0.3 in (8 mm) in length. In Europe, and also introduced and established in California, lives the slightly longer *H. blackwalli*, the mouse spider, so called because of its velvety coat of mouse-colored hairs. The author occasionally sees the mouse spider on the walls of his own home, its wanderings temporarily suspended by the sudden switching on of a light. If disturbed, they can demonstrate quite a turn of speed.

DAYLIGHT HUNTERS

Whereas we seldom see spiders of the previous group, the free-living, lycosid wolf spiders are much more likely to be seen since they are daylight hunters. Typical of the wolf spiders is the arrangement of the second row of eyes, with two large, central eyes looking forward from the somewhat

Herpyllus blackwalli (right) is a nocturnal hunter. It is common in houses and outbuildings in Europe. This female was found beneath a pile of flowerpots protecting her egg sac.

elevated head region of the cephalothorax, giving them good forward vision; and a second pair of large eyes, one on each side and set farther back on the head, looking up to give them improved all-round vision.

Members of the genus *Lycosa* from Australia, Europe and the U.S.A. are often handsomely marked and may exceed 1.5 in (40 mm) in length. *Lycosa* is not found in the British Isles, but occurs in southern Europe, including Italy from whence comes its common name of tarantula, for these are the true tarantulas. Many are active hunters in grassland habitats, though as we have already seen, a number live in burrows. Although they feed mainly upon insects, they will take other prey. An individual *Lycosa ammophila* from Florida, for example, was seen to dispatch a juvenile *Anolis carolinensis* lizard twice its size. Fireflies are a source of food for some species of *Lycosa*, and one would suppose that with their good eyesight the spiders would be drawn to them by the light they produce. It turns out that this is not the case, for though the flashes of light produced by the fireflies may attract the spiders to the general area occupied by the insects, it is the vibrations they produce by which the lycosas find them.

Closer to home, since they are often found in suburban backyards, are the brown and black members of the genus *Pardosa*, which occur both in Europe and the U.S.A. There are at least two different species in the author's garden, recognizable by the fact that in one the female carries a faintly blue-green egg sac, while the other carries a white one at a slightly later time of year. These little spiders, most of them less than 0.4 in (10 mm) long, run around in the warm sun taking any small insect prey that comes within pouncing distance.

DEADLY FISHERMEN

It is also possible to see the members of the genus *Dolomedes*, called swamp spiders in the British Isles and fisher spiders in the U.S.A. These spiders are quite large by true spider standards, rivaling the large lycosas in size. They are able to run across the surface of ponds or slow-moving streams, where most species prey upon insects or other small arthropods that have fallen into the water. As often as not, the spider will sit on a leaf of some water plant with some of its legs resting on the water surface to pick up the ripples generated by some hapless creature which has fallen in. Some species have even been seen to take small fish and tadpoles, thus the common name, which the spider pounces on when they come too near to the surface where it is lurking. Some American *Dolomedes* have been observed "fishing" for their prey, dipping the end of their legs into the water and waving them around to attract small fish.

THE NOCTURNAL HUNTER

This spectacular-looking spider, *Dysdera crocata*, is a nocturnal hunter that specializes in woodlice as prey. The latter have very tough exoskeletons, and this accounts for *Dysdera*'s enormous fangs, which are capable of giving humans a painful bite if they handle the spider carelessly.

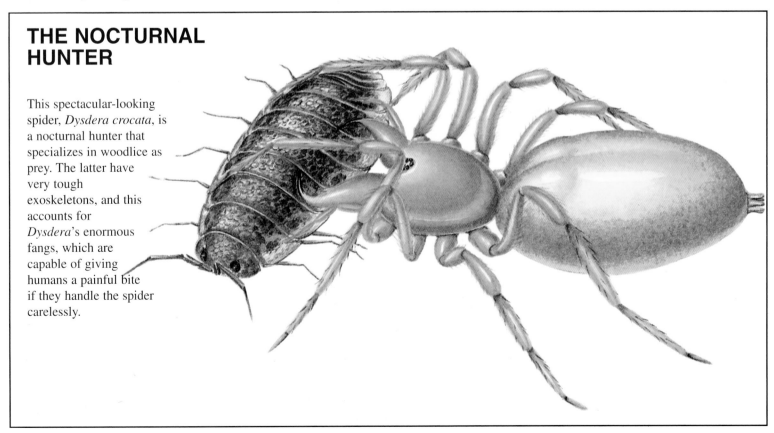

Perhaps more interesting than the lycosids from the point of view of their hunting methods are the members of the family *Pisauridae*. They resemble the lycosids in general body form, though the head is not so elevated and the posterior eyes are not quite so large. Despite this, they are very successful daylight hunters in their own right. Most likely to be encountered are the fisher spiders, hunters of insects on low vegetation.

Another family which are characteristically large-eyed daylight hunters are the lynx spiders, the *Oxyopidae*. They hunt actively upon vegetation, finding their prey visually and pouncing on it. They are mainly tropical spiders. There is only a single rare species in the British Isles. The U.S.A. is home to the lynx spider *Peucetia viridans*, which is widespread and common in the southern states. It is the female that you are most likely to find, sitting guarding her egg sac or feeding upon recently caught prey.

Green lynx spiders of the genus Peucetia *are widespread in the world's tropical and subtropical regions, where they hunt actively on plants for their prey. This example from southern Africa (above) has caught one of millions of winged termites that were swarming at the time the picture was taken. The widespread New World species* P. viridans *is seen here (right) in Costa Rica with its prey, an assassin bug, itself an efficient predator.*

JUMPING SPIDERS

When we come to the jumping spiders of the family *Salticidae*, we reach the peak of perfection in the art of the hunting spider. Jumping spiders are lovers of the sun and therefore reach their greatest numbers in the world's tropical forests, where their brilliant hues make them veritable jewels of the arthropod world. They also spread into the temperate zones, where they tend to be more drab, though not exclusively so. They have the largest eyes of all spiders relative to their size; the center pair on the front of the head has the appearance of a pair of car headlights when the spider looks at you, and look at you it will if it catches your movement. It is in fact quite uncanny the way it swivels its head around to peer at you, as if it is sizing you up as a meal, but its little face makes it among the most endearing of spiders. It is this central pair of eyes with which it focuses on its prey, once its movements have been picked up by the other eyes. The slightly smaller eyes, one on each side of the large eyes, give the spider binocular vision and it uses these to calculate the distance to its prey.

Jumping spiders can recognize prey up to about 14 times their own body length away, and although they can jump on it from this distance, they usually try to move stealthily closer to improve their chances of a successful capture. The spider anchors its dragline, which is pulled out behind it as it makes the final leap upon its ill-fated victim, which is immediately dispatched with a lethal bite. Salticids are not very large spiders, few of them exceeding 0.6 in (15 mm) in length, but despite this they are able to take prey many times their own size.

There are a number of primitive species of jumping spider, however, which still use webs. Two such spiders, *Spartaeus spinimanus* from Singapore and *S. thailandicus* from Thailand, built sheet webs on the surface of tree trunks. The spiders spend most of their lives hidden from their enemies beneath these webs, and they catch mainly moths on or close to the web by lunging at them, rather than jumping on them like the rest of the salticids. Any prey which lands on the web is grabbed from beneath through the silk and immobilized with poison. The spider then emerges from beneath the web and carries the prey back below the web to feed.

THE "CANNIBAL" SPIDER

Portia fimbriata from Australia has been seen to be able to enter and move around in the webs of other spiders. Here, by the use of aggressive mimicry, that is by vibrating the web with its legs and palps much like a prey insect, it is able to lure the host spider toward it as a possible meal. Outside the area of its web, it has also been seen to stalk and capture other species of jumping spider, which apparently are unable to recognize that it is a danger to them. It seems that this species actually feeds more upon other spiders than it does on insects, though it has been seen to take the latter both on and off its own web and from the webs of other spiders. It even takes advantage of other spiders by eating their eggs whenever it finds them.

Jumping spiders show an amazing diversity of color and pattern from species to species, and despite their dimunitive size are capable of taking quite large insect prey. Both the Plexippus (below left) from Kenya and the unidentified salticid species (below right) from Brazil's dwindling Atlantic-coast rainforest have caught bush crickets several times larger than themselves.

THE WEB-BUILDERS

Mention the word "spider," and most people immediately think of it in its web, for of course many species depend entirely upon their silken trap as a source of food. Say "spider's web," and most of us immediately picture the orb web of the garden spider, but of course this is only one of a multitude of different arrangements of silk which spiders have evolved in order to trap their prey. The number of individual web designs that have evolved is so great that we only have space to consider a few of the most basic designs, together with some of the most extreme and perhaps most interesting ones.

GROUND-LEVEL FUNNELS AND TUBES

We have seen that many of the most primitive spiders of the *Mygalomorphae* live in silk-lined burrows from which they emerge to pounce on their prey. A number of them, including the notorious funnel web spiders of the genus *Atrax* from Australia, have extended the silk out from the burrow and over the adjoining surfaces in the form of a broadmouthed funnel. Insects walking upon this sheet of silk trigger an immediate response from the spider, which sits in wait at the narrowest part of the funnel.

Although not many people are likely to come across *Atrax*, most will be familiar with the common agelenid house spiders of the genus *Tegenaria*,

VARIATIONS ON A THEME

Not all spiders build orb webs; some make simpler webs, while others make them more complex.
1 *Episinus* traps insects that walk between the two sticky lines she has attached to the soil surface.
2 The Australian black house spider *Ixeuticus robustus* builds a funnel containing strands of hackled-band silk.
3 *Wixia ectypa* from the U.S.A. builds a tripline web on trees and sits at the center in wait for its prey.

4 The ladder of nonsticky silk in the web of *Scoloderus cordatus* from the U.S.A. rubs the scales off moths' wings so that the latter tumble down and are caught on the sticky spirals of the orb below.
5 *Theridion saxatile* from Europe builds a scaffold web just above the ground. Insects walking on the soil are trapped by the sticky vertical lines.

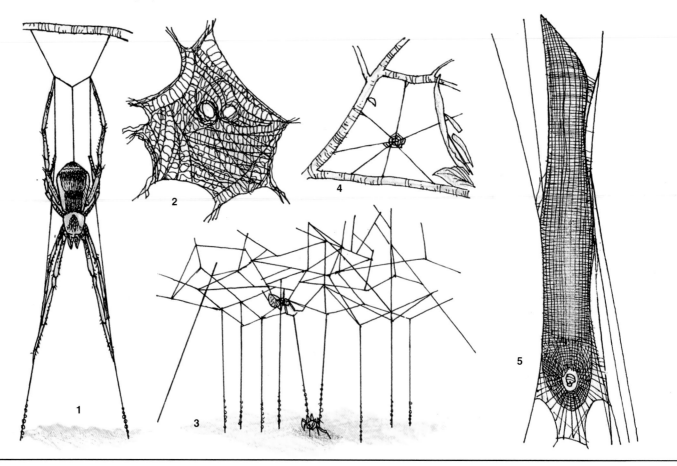

which occur both in Europe and the U.S.A., and *T. domestica*, which has become established in parts of Australia. Most readers' experience of them will be of the wandering males in search of a mate, who end up falling into the bathtub, from which they are unable to escape without human intervention as they cannot get a grip on the tub's smooth sides. The females are not wanderers and spend their lives in a tubular silk retreat in a dark corner. From this retreat extends a broad sheet web, onto which wandering insects stumble with obviously fatal results.

SHEETS AND SCAFFOLDS

Other types of spider have taken the sheet web off the ground and support it on plants, sometimes in the form of a hammock or a dome. This type of web is typical of the family *Linyphiidae*, whose members are the great "balloonists" of northern temperate regions. The web consists essentially of a broad sheet, above which is a maze of scaffolding lines, with a smaller number of lines running from below the sheet to keep it in place. The spider hangs below the sheet waiting for insects to blunder into the scaffold lines above and fall onto the sheet. Attracted by the movements, the spider then rushes up onto the sheet to capture its prey before it escapes, since there is no sticky silk to trap it.

The *Theridiidae* build a web that consists of an aerial sheet web minus the sheet, so it is usually referred to as a scaffold web. Within the scaffold are strategically placed lines of sticky silk, and insects blundering through the scaffold lines become attached to them and cannot escape. Some species build the scaffold just above the ground, with the sticky lines stretched vertically and attached to the surface. If a crawling insect walks into one of these, it becomes stuck, and its struggles cause the silk to break at a point close to the ground. The trapped insect is immediately pulled off the ground by the contracting silk, whereupon the female spider descends from her lair in the scaffold, grabs her victim, wraps it and then delivers the fatal bite.

Agelenid spiders build sheet webs with a funnel-shaped lair at the center. A female Agelena labyrinthica *from Europe sits at the entrance to her lair (below) and waits for a victim to stumble upon her dew-covered sheet web, whereupon she will rush out and pounce.*

It is not easy to produce good photographs of spider webs since the silk is very thin and does not show up well. There are exceptions, however, and the conditions in which the web of the South African Gasteracantha falcicornis *(right) were photographed, i.e., a gloomy forest and lighting by natural backlighting, gave a perfect result. Although the web is slightly damaged with use, it still shows the main components of a typical araneid orb web.*

Spiders will only spin a new web when it is absolutely necessary. From the amount of damage and general untidiness at the center of the web of Nephila inaurata *(right), from Kenya, it is clear that she will soon have to construct a new one.*

ORB WEBS

Although many people may be relatively unfamiliar with the foregoing types of web, few are unaware of the existence of the orb web. The construction of orb webs by both the cribellate family *Uloboridae* and the ecribellate *Araneidae* appears on present evidence to be due to convergent evolution; i.e., similar structures have been arrived at independently in the two groups as an answer to the same problem, namely how to capture prey more efficiently. The final orb-web structure is very similar in the two groups, but whereas in the *Araneidae* the spirals are made from viscid silk from the

spinnerets, in the *Uloboridae* they are made from cribellar silk laid down over a warp of spinneret silk.

Prey is taken in a similar way by both families, in that once it is caught in the web, the spider rushes up to it and wraps it in silk to subdue it. However, whereas the *Araneidae* inject their prey with venom before wrapping it, poison glands are much reduced or absent in the uloborids, so they throw silk over the prey before they move in to wrap it.

Since the orb web has twice evolved independently in this way, it must clearly confer a number of advantages, so what are they? In the first place, with only a relatively

small outlay of material, it forms a flexible, strong structure covering a large area, making it highly efficient at catching flying insects. Second, it needs very few points of attachment and may be positioned in any plane, though of course individual families tend to stick to a particular plane for their webs. The third point is that signals from trapped prey, or a spider of the opposite sex, can be sent straight to the spider, who can then follow the same line back to the source of the signal. Finally, the careful geometrical arrangement of the capture threads and the spokes allows the spider to move around the web on the latter without itself becoming trapped on the former.

CATCHING FLYING INSECTS

A lot of evidence points to the fact that flying insects can actually see

FENDING OFF THE BOMBADIER

Some araneid spiders have managed to learn how to handle the extremely offensive bombadier beetles. These creatures eject a jet of hot, irritating liquid which repels most attackers. Spiders of the genus *Argiope*, however, approach the beetle cautiously, wrap it in silk and then leave it until it has exhausted its supply of spray before eating it.

ARANEID ORB-WEB CONSTRUCTION

1 The spider starts the web's framework with a bridge line between two adjacent uprights, either by walking between them or by using the breeze to carry the silk.
2 The spider tightens the bridge line and then strengthens it by walking backward and forward over it, laying down extra strands of silk.
3 The spider next produces a loop of silk, which hangs below the bridge line. The spider descends to the center of this, then drops another line down vertically to a lower twig.
4 The spider now pulls the vertical line down and anchors it to produce the layout shown here.

The point where the three lines join is the web's center.
5 It completes the main frame of the web by spinning a number of lines to finish the outer framework, which is connected to the center by some more radial threads.
6 It adds many more radial threads to the web, and when they are complete, it returns to the center, where it lays down a few turns of strengthening spirals.
7 Starting from just outside the strengthening spirals, the spider now walks from radius to radius in an outward direction, laying down the temporary nonsticky spinals.
8 The spider now reverses direction and, following the temporary spirals, lays down the sticky spirals, demolishing the former as it proceeds to the center.

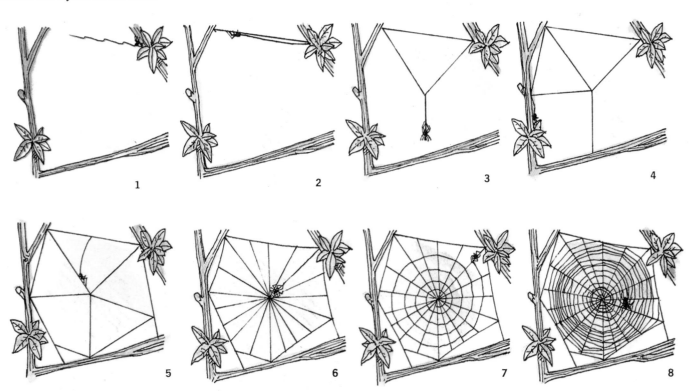

LIGHT-REFLECTING WEBS

There has been a lot of speculation about the role of the zigzag pattern of silk, the stabilimentum, which is added to the center of the web of many orb weavers, such as species of *Argiope*. At one time it was thought that the stabilimentum, which stands out very clearly, was there to prevent birds from flying into and badly damaging the web. Recent research has, however, come up with a much more plausible answer. Whereas the silk which makes up most of the web of these spiders is a poor reflector of ultraviolet light, that which makes up the stabilimentum reflects it very efficiently. Flowers reflect ultraviolet very well, in order to attract pollinating insects to them, so it looks as if the role of the stabilimentum is to attract insects to the web, by mimicking a flower.

The shiny, white, light-reflecting threads that form the stabilimentum are especially characteristic of the orb webs of araneid spiders of the genus Argiope. *The nature of the stabilimentum varies with the stage of development of the spider. The web of* A. argentata *(left), from the New World, shows the stabilimentum of an immature spider while the web of* A. lobata *(right), from Africa, shows that of the mature spider.*

spiders' webs quite clearly and are thus able to take steps to avoid them. For example, some recent research in the U.S.A. has involved videotaping mosquitoes and fruit flies flying toward webs suspended in frames in a wind tunnel. This has shown that the insects are able to detect the web up to 4 in (100 mm) away and can see individual threads at 0.25–0.5 in (6–12 mm) distance. It was also noted that if any hole in the web had not been repaired, the insect would fly through it.

Spiders seem to be aware that insects can see their webs, for an examination of the way in which orb weavers position their webs indicates that they make a choice about exactly where they are placed. Those species which are active in the day in good light have to build their webs close to bushes or other structures that act as a background against which their webs are less visible. Spiders which are nocturnal or live in the forest depths, where light is very dim, are able to exploit a much greater volume of potential prey-trapping air space, since they do not have to build their webs against a close background.

Many, but not all, orb-web spiders sit in the center of the web as they wait for prey to fly into it. The hub where they sit is sometimes placed above the web's center, and it has now been shown that this is, perhaps obviously, because it takes the spider longer to run uphill than it does for it to run down. Thus it can cover the shorter distance uphill from the hub of the web in much the same time it takes to run the longer distance downward.

The female orb-web spider Argiope lobata *(above) from Africa has just caught and finished wrapping a grasshopper that has inadvertently flown into her web. She may either eat it immediately or leave it hanging in its silken shroud until she is hungry.*

THE SPECIALISTS

A number of spiders do not fit into the simple system of short-sighted hunters, active hunters and web-builders, but have evolved fascinating lifestyles of their own. We shall consider a number of these in this section.

THE WATER SPIDER

It is not possible to discuss the spiders as a whole without considering the unique way of life of *Argyroneta aquatica*, the water spider. *Argyroneta* comes from Europe and Asia and spends the whole of its life beneath the surface of ponds and lakes. They are not very big spiders, about 0.5 in (12 mm) long, are basically brown in color, and build a thimble-shaped underwater lair out of silk. This lair is first constructed as a slightly curved platform which is anchored to surrounding water plants. The spider then swims to the surface, where it collects a bubble of air which it holds in its hind legs before making its way back to the silk platform. The bubble is released beneath the platform, rises up beneath it and is trapped, increasing its curvature at the same time. More silk may be added to increase the strength of the lair before a further series of trips to the surface eventually fills the lair, which by now has assumed its final thimble shape. As the oxygen is used up by the spider, it is replaced at intervals with fresh bubbles from the surface. Carbon dioxide produced by the spider simply diffuses out into the water and is dispersed.

Once the lair is complete, the spider sits in it and awaits any arthropod which happens to swim by. If one does, then the spider swoops out of the lair, grasps it in her legs and pulls it toward her jaws to deliver the fatal bite. Water spiders will also take struggling insects from the surface of the water, suggesting that the former senses the vibrations of the latter. She may also leave her lair at night and go hunting prey such as small shrimp and insect larvae from the bottom of the pond. Whatever she catches, the water spider always returns with it to the lair to feed. The reason for this is quite simple. You will remember that spiders digest their prey outside their body by pouring digestive juices onto it. If the water spider did this while she was still in the water, rather than in the air bubble in the lair, then the digestive juices would be so diluted by the water that they would become totally ineffective.

The lair is the center of the water spider's life, for not only does she feed and rest there, but she also mates and lays her eggs there. The only time that these spiders leave water is as babies, when they disperse by ballooning, or on the odd occasion when they get wet as a result of bad waterproofing. In the latter circumstance, they must leave the water in order to dry off, otherwise they would become waterlogged.

LAIR CONSTRUCTION IN THE WATER SPIDER

The spider first chooses a suitable area of water weeds within which to construct its bell-shaped lair (**1**). Having done so, it constructs a slightly curved, circular pad of elastic silk, which is attached to the stems of the surrounding plants (**2**). The spider now swims to the surface and traps a bubble of air, which it holds between its hind legs. It now uses the other legs to walk or swim down to the silken pad (**3**). It releases the bubble beneath the pad, and the bubble is trapped, at the same time increasing the pad's upward curvature (**4**). The process is repeated time and again with intermediate pauses to extend and strengthen the pad, which begins to assume its domed shape. Once the lair is complete and filled with air, the spider climbs inside, leaving it only to catch prey or to replenish the air as the oxygen in it becomes exhausted (**5**).

  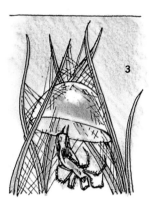 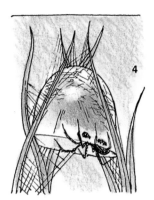 

WATERY SPIDERS

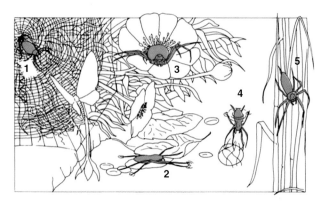

Although many species of spiders avoid damp and watery places, there are many others to whom such environments are their natural home. Some depend on water as a retreat from danger or as a source of food, while others are simply attracted to the waterside vegetation, which is a good source of insect victims. *Argiope bruennichi* (1) is a European spider which often constructs its large orb web in the tall vegetation around ponds and ditches. The various species of *Dolomedes* (2) from the U.S.A. and Europe spend their lives on or near the water surface, feeding on small water organisms, or even fish in the case of one American species. Alternatively, they may prey on

insects which have had the misfortune to fall in. The crab spider *Misumena vatia* (3), which is also found on both sides of the Atlantic, is likely to be found on flowers in almost any type of environment, waiting to ambush its prey. The Eurasian water spider *Argyroneta aquatica* (4) is the only spider that habitually lives and hunts below the water surface; here it is depicted with the tip of its abdomen out of the water as it replenishes its air supply. Crab spiders of the genus *Tibellus* (5) are much more elongated than the typical forms and generally lie in wait for their prey stretched out along a blade of grass or a plant stem.

Scale
1 *Argiope bruennichi*, ⁹⁄₁₆ in (15 mm).
2 *Dolomedes*, ⅞ in (20 mm).
3 *Misumena vatia* ⅜ in (10 mm).
4 *Argyroneta aquatica* ⁹⁄₁₆ in (14 mm).
5 *Tibellus* ⅜ in (10 mm).

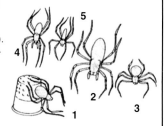

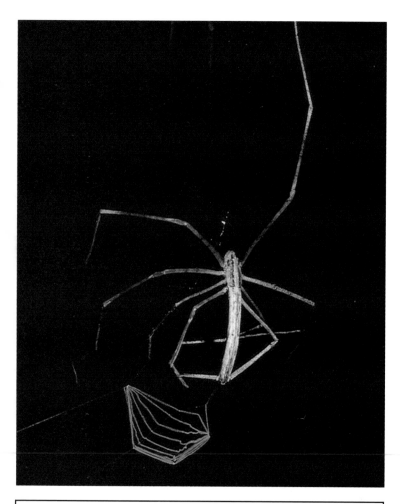

BOLAS SPIDERS

Bolas spiders are araneids that have given up the use of the orb web and adopted instead a very specialized form of prey capture.

1 The spider hangs from a single line, holding a short thread on the end of which is a globule of sticky silk. When an insect such as a moth approaches, it begins to whirl its bolas.

2 With the moth now in range, the spider shoots the bolas out in its direction. As the sticky globule touches the moth, it sticks to it. The moth is stopped in midflight, whereupon the spider reels it in and dispatches it with a fatal bite.

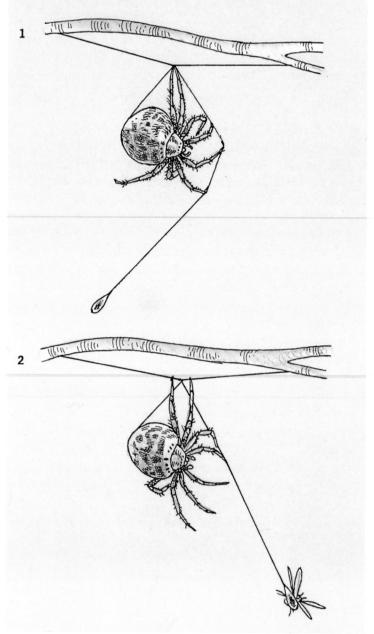

INVISIBLE ATTRACTORS

A photographer was photographing *Dinopus guatemalensis* in Costa Rica. He had gone out in the early evening, when these spiders begin their night's trapping, and had found one setting itself up in readiness with its net. No sooner had the spider gotten into position, about 12 in (300 mm) above the ground, when a moth appeared out of nowhere and the spider took it. Having not yet taken enough pictures, the photographer took the moth away from the spider, whereupon it set itself up again in the catching position. Within a very short time, another moth appeared and was immediately trapped. There were no moths around at all while the spider was unprepared for catching prey; they only appeared when it was hanging ready with its net. This indicates the production of some form of attractant by the spider.

NET-THROWING SPIDERS

This, along with ogre-faced, retiarius and stick, are the common names given to the amazing spiders of the cribellate family *Dinopidae*. These spiders are tropical in distribution, thus they are not found in Europe, but they are found in Australia and in the southeastern states, especially Florida, where the species *Dinopus spinosus* has been fairly extensively studied. As the name perhaps implies, these spiders do not wait for the insect to come to the web, but instead take the web to the insect.

First, the spider manufactures a scaffold of dry silk and on it begins to weave a rectangular web of thick bands of cribellar silk along with strands of other types of silk laid down on a framework of dragline silk. This rectangular web is of such a size that its four corners can be held comfortably by one of each of the spider's four front legs when they are at full stretch. Once the rectangle is complete, the spider, holding each corner by one of the front legs, cuts it free from the scaffold. Amazingly, it now collapses to about one-tenth of its original size. Recent research indicates that this is due both to the fact that some of the silk strands are produced in a highly stretched state, while others coil up as the web contracts.

The net-throwing spider Dinopus quatemalensis *(opposite left) typically constructs and uses its web during the hours of darkness. At dawn it either destroys the web or leaves it to be used again the next night. This individual is seen at night in Costa Rica in the act of constructing its net. A strand of new silk can clearly be seen running from the spinnerets on the tip of its abdomen.*

The spider can now use its "handheld" web to net prey in one of two ways. It can sit on the dry strands of its web, head down, and as insects fly past open up the net to its full size in their flight path so that they blunder into it. It is thought that insects may be attracted to these spiders by the pheromones produced by the latter. Once trapped, the web may be shaken to enmesh the prey further before the spider wraps it in more silk and begins to feed. The second trapping method involves the spider moving to that part of the web which is attached to the ground or other surface on which walking insects may pass by. Here the spider hangs head down in such a position that it can just touch the ground with the tips of its front legs. It now waits, and if an insect walks past beneath it, the spider opens up its net and drops it over its victim.

THE BOLAS SPIDERS

Having gone to the trouble of evolving that wonderful prey-trapping structure, the orb web, it is odd to find that a number of araneids have given it up and use other methods of prey capture. One such group is the bolas spiders, which are known from Africa, Australia and North America, but not from Europe. They are globular spiders which spend the day clinging motionless to a twig or leaf toward the end of a branch on a shrub, for they are essentially nocturnal hunters. As night falls, the spider lays down a line of dry silk between two adjacent twigs or leaves and then moves to the center of it. In this position, the spider now produces its bolas, a length of silk about 1 in (25 mm) long, on the end of which is a globule of viscid silk. Hanging from the dry line with the bolas hanging from a

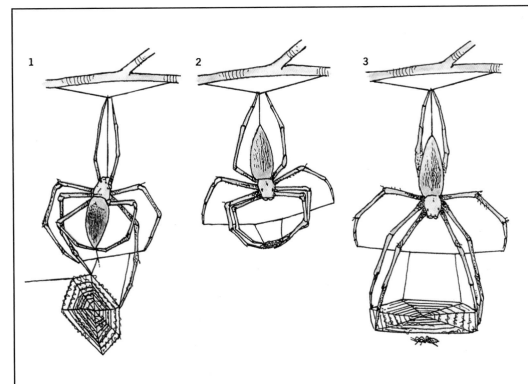

NET-THROWING SPIDERS

The *Dinopidae* do not sit in their webs like other spiders. Instead, they hold them and throw them over their prey.
1 The spider attaches a framework to surrounding vegetation and builds the web itself, which is made from contractile silk, onto it.
2 The spider hangs from its frame web, head down just above the ground, with its net held in the first two pairs of legs.
3 As an insect walks below it, the spider stretches the net and drops it over its victim.

The most noticeable point about spitting spiders is the extremely elevated head, which houses the modified venom glands which produce the gum. This feature is very apparent on the female Scytodes (left) from Chile.

A DEADLY EMBRACE

Although not strictly speaking bolas spiders, there are some closely related spiders which have dispensed with the use of silk for trapping prey altogether. One such spider is *Taczanowskia* from South America. She sets herself up in much the same way as the bolas spider, without the bolas, facing downwind and with the first and second pairs of legs partly spread. When a moth or other insect approaches, the spider spreads her legs wide as soon as she detects it, seizes it with a sudden grab and grasps it to her before wrapping it and feeding. The way in which the spider sits, with the breeze blowing from behind her and the approach of insects from the front, indicates that these spiders may well produce a chemical attractant to draw the prey toward them.

front leg, the spider now waits for a flying insect to pass within range. If one does, the spider whirls the bolas so that the sticky globule on the end comes into contact with the prey, which is stopped in full flight, the elasticity of the silk absorbing the sudden shock. The spider then reels in the line and begins to feed.

SPITTING SPIDERS

Spiders of the family *Scytodidae*, the spitting spiders, have given up the use of silk to capture their prey, though they use it to wrap them. The cephalothorax of these spiders has a noticeable hump, which contains modified venom glands which produce large amounts of a special secretion that solidifies on contact with solid objects. *Sytodes thoracic* has, as a result of man's influence, spread through much of the world, where it hunts at night on the walls and ceilings of houses. It moves stealthily around until it finds a suitable prey, which is approached to within about a body length, when the spider appears to give a sudden jerk. What has occurred is too fast for the human eye to see, but results in a completely immobilized prey that can be picked up, wrapped and eaten when the spider is ready. During the sudden jerk, the spider has spat two streams of gum, one from each jaw, over the insect. As it spits out the gum, it oscillates its jaws so that a zigzag of sticky gum attaches to both the insect and the surface on which it is standing, anchoring it firmly in the process. So much gum is produced that there is a noticeable lowering of the hump on the cephalothorax as the gum glands are emptied.

SPIDER-EATING SPIDERS

Some spiders specialize in other species of spider as their food source. They are not, as you might expect, large spiders which prey upon smaller ones, but in the main small spiders which catch others by stealth and the use of a powerful venom. One family, the *Mimetidae*, are almost exclusively spider feeders, only rarely taking insect prey. They walk carefully and gently into the webs, where they wait until the host spider wanders too close. They grasp the host's leg and bite it, and the powerful poison immediately kills the host.

Whereas the mimetids are specialists in spider prey, a number of spiders of species scattered throughout the spider families will take other

A SPITTING SPIDER CATCHING PREY

The only way to record the spitting spider's method of catching its prey is a high-speed movie camera. Here we can only appreciate the end product, for the spider has already spat two streams of gum, one from each fang, over the fly and efficiently anchored it to the substrate. The waviness of the lines of gum is explained by the fact that as it spat the spider rapidly oscillated its head from side to side.

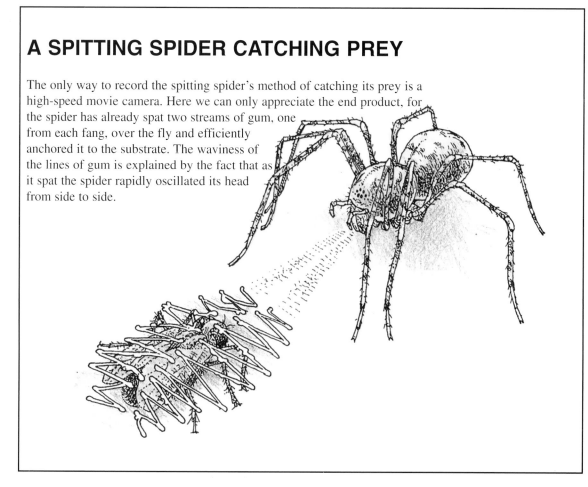

Although a number of spiders prey specifically upon other species of spider, occasionally a spider may become the victim of another member of its own species. The two spiders involved here are males of the European species Meta segmentata *(below).*

spiders when they are available. One such spider that you might see performing its evil deeds is the primitive six-eyed daddy longlegs, *Pholcus phalangioides*. This is found in human habitation virtually worldwide as long as the ambient temperature does not get below about 64°F (10°C). It lives in its own nonsticky web, where it traps prey by throwing silk over it and then wrapping it up to immobilize it. It also enters the webs of other spiders and preys upon their prey, their eggs, and sometimes the host spiders themselves. This behavior is very similar to that of the web-building salticids of the genus *Portia*, which themselves will feed upon *Pholcus* given the chance.

On entering the web of a possible prey spider, they both employ what is known as aggressive mimicry, that is, they manipulate the web in a manner similar to that of a trapped insect. This attracts the web's owner to within reach of the waiting jaws of the predatory invader. These invaders do not, however, always get their own way, for on occasions they make the mistake of entering the web of a spider that is larger and stronger than themselves, in which case they end up as a meal for the host.

KLEPTOPARASITISM

The prefix klepto-, perhaps more familiar in the word kleptomania, comes from the Greek *kleptes*, a thief. Kleptoparasites, therefore, are animals which steal food from other spiders' webs that has not yet been eaten. This distinguishes kleptoparasites that effectively compete with the spider from commensal animals which live in or near the spider's web and help to keep it clean by feeding on scraps of food which the spider has discarded. As you might expect, there is a hazy zone between these two, since a commensal might often take as unwanted something that the spider has not actually finished. Kleptoparasites include the scorpion-flies of the order *Mecoptera*, certain species of bird, such as humming-birds, which hover by the web to remove the spider's prey, and above all, other species of spider.

One theridiid genus in particular, *Argyrodes*, has adopted the role of the kleptoparasite. Some argyrods are not choosy about which host they pick on and may be found in a range of different webs, while others are more particular and may be restricted to just a few species. They are small spiders and appear to have evolved the ability to move quietly and unobtrusively around their host's web, helping themselves to its prey, even to the extent of feeding from it at the same time as the host. One species, *Argyrodes trigonum*, is known to be both a kleptoparasite of and to feed upon the bowl-and-doily spider, *Frontinella pyramitela*. During the summer months in the U.S.,A. trigonum may inhabit up to 20 percent of the available bowl-and-doilys' webs, where it has either caused the death or departure of the host. The bowl-and-doily spiders appear to be able to recognize that the invader is a "wrong'un," for if they make contact with it, say with the tip of a front leg, they immediately retreat in apparent alarm.

Having caught itself a meal, a spider may then find that it has to share it. The scorpion-fly Panorpa communis *(below right), for example, is a scavenger and here is making a meal of a moth trapped by an orb-web spider.* Argyrodes elevatus *from Brazil belongs to a genus whose members excel in web robbery.*

Here (below left), one is seen sharing a meal with a huge female Nephila clavipes. *On occasions a spider that normally catches its own food will steal from another. The* Xysticus *female (opposite) is doing just that, from the web of a garden spider.*

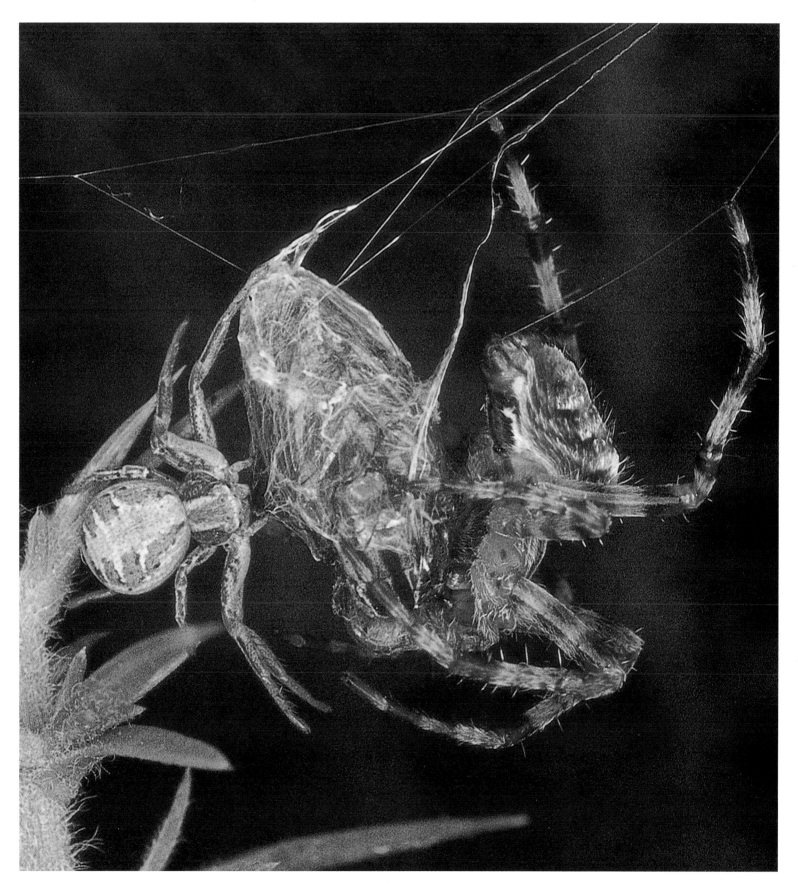

SOCIAL SPIDERS

You might be surprised to learn that, especially in the world's tropical and subtropical zones, a number of spiders have opted for a social existence. The degree to which they cooperate with one another differs, however, from species to species, from an individual spider living in its own web to a series of individuals sharing a web and the food that is attracted and captured. What, therefore, are the advantages for a spider of living a social existence? In the case of the orb web, flying insects are able to detect the presence of a web as they approach it and take appropriate avoiding action to prevent being caught. If only a single web blocks the insect's flight path, then a quick swerve will take it out of harm's way. Imagine, however, the situation where a number of spiders have built their webs in a close-knit group. In this instance, the swerving insect is likely to find its way blocked by a second web, and if it can avoid this, by a third, and so on. Clearly, an insect's maneuverability in flight has its limitations, and having flown into a social group, it is likely to end up in one of the webs.

The less cooperative of the social spiders include species which are facultatively communal, meaning they can survive quite happily in their own isolated web or in a community, and they probably represent an early stage in the evolution toward a fully social group. A good example is the American uloborid *Philoponella oweni*. If there are plenty of sites available for a web, this spider will opt for a lone existence in its own web. If, however, building sites are in short supply and plenty of insect prey is available, they will form a communal group. There is no cooperation between these spiders, each living within its own web in the community and repelling any other members of the group which attempt to enter its web.

COLONIES OF WEBS

In the closely related *P. republicans*, things have evolved a little farther. Each spider within the group builds its own web, but it may enter the web of another to help subdue and wrap a very large insect. Where two or more spiders are present in this situation, there will be a brief altercation before the strongest takes over and feeds on the prey. In this species, if the number of flying insects in the area of the colony drops for any reason, the distance between the individual webs is increased and in conditions of extreme prey reduction, the whole colony may move to a new site.

Sociability in the spider has probably evolved gradually with, in its early stages, the young building their webs close to their mother's web, but remaining independent of her. This is the case for the araneid Cyrtophora hirta *(left), which lives in woodland in Australia.*

The degree to which social spiders tolerate each other's presence is amply illustrated by Metapeira spinipes *(above), seen here in Mexico, where its webs covered bushes along a roadside for a distance of hundreds of yards.* Cyrtophora moluccensis *(right) from New Guinea is closely related to* C. hirta *(see previous page), but has a much more highly developed social structure, with adjoining webs using structural threads in common.*

Truly social spiders not only benefit from the fact that their composite webs act as one large web, which increases its overall efficiency in catching prey. They can also collectively drive off spider-hunting or parasitic wasps, and females can share the upbringing of the young spiders. Some recent research on the Panamanian social theridiid spider, *Anelosimus eximius*, which lives in colonies containing anything between 1000 and 10,000 members, has shown that it benefits in yet another way. When an insect becomes trapped in the web, it is attacked by spiders which are nearby. The larger the insect, the greater the disturbance, and therefore the more spiders are attracted to attack it. This allows the tiny 0.25-in (6-mm)-long spiders to attack prey up to 12 times their own size, prey which would easily make its escape from a single web with its lone occupant. Being able to take advantage of such large prey in its turn provides food for a large number of small spiders.

DEFENSIVE ADAPTATIONS

Small animals such as spiders and scorpions
are always at risk from larger predators,
and they have therefore evolved a number of
ploys to protect themselves. A number of
spiders and most scorpions dig burrows, in
which they spend most of their lives. They
come out only to hunt or, in the case of
scorpions and male spiders, to find a mate.
Active defense is rare in spiders, though
some release stinging hairs, and at least one
has the ability to spit venom. Some spiders
that live in the vicinity of water can escape
their enemies by diving below the surface.
Passive defense is much more common, and
many spider species either have camouflage
or can mimic inanimate objects such as
flowers or dead leaves.

Caerostris mitralis *from
Madagascar conceals itself from
its enemies by remaining
motionless during daylight hours
on a twig, where it resembles a
protruding bump or driedup bud.*

BURROWING SPIDERS

One way of overcoming the problems of extreme variations in temperature or humidity, or to keep out of the way of predatory animals, is to live underground in a burrow. The burrowing lifestyle is typical of many of the mygalomorphs.

TRAP-DOOR BURROWS

The supreme burrowing spiders are to be found among the mygalomorphs, and their retreats show some very clear deviations from a simple hole in the ground. We have already seen how they make use of them as a hideaway from which to pounce on passing prey, so we will not dwell on this point but look more closely at the protective function of the burrow. The main enemies of these spiders are wasps (which sting them and use them as food for their young), scorpions and large centipedes. These are all capable of entering the spider's burrow, and therefore the spider has developed a number of amazing ways in which to avoid capture. Perhaps the simplest of these is just to hang tightly onto the trap door that often covers the entrance to the spider's burrow.

The retreat of the Australian mygalomorph, *Lampropodus iridescens*, has adaptations both to climatic factors and to predators. Instead of a trap door, the burrow is open at the top, and around it is a raised palisade of vegetable material which acts as a flood defense. Halfway down the flask-shaped main shaft is a side shaft into which the spider just fits. Across the entrance to this is a trap door, which can be swung into position by

DEFENSIVE PLOYS

1 The simplest form of escape for a burrowing spider is to have a trap door that drops over the entrance once its owner is inside. The spider may also hold the trap door shut by gripping the underside in its jaws and bracing its legs against the side of the burrow.

2 *Stanwellia nebulosa* from Australia has both a trap door and a specially balanced pebble which the spider pulls down behind itself as it retreats.

3 The American *Cyclocosmia truncata* has both a trap door and an armored plate over the end of its abdomen that fits tightly against the sides of the burrow, protecting it against an attack from anything entering the burrow behind it.

the tenant spider to hide her from intruders. The silk-lined side chamber with its tight-fitting lid also forms an air pocket in the eventuality of the main shaft becoming flooded. *Myrmekiaphila* from the southeastern states has a very similar, but tubular, burrow, but it lacks the side chamber and instead has a normal trap door.

FALSE-BOTTOMED BURROWS

Another way is to have a false bottom to the burrow, below which the spider hides out of sight of its enemies. This is the ploy of *Anidiops* from Australia. She has a silk cuff part of the way down the burrow, and if threatened she retreats below it, pulling it across the burrow behind her as she goes. Between the cuff and the burrow wall, she has stuffed the remains of prey and other debris, which falls on top of the cuff as it closes,

giving the impression of the messy bottom of the burrow. The pebble spider, *Stanwellia nebulosa*, also from Australia, digs a side chamber partway down her shaft and into it places a carefully chosen pebble. When she retreats into her burrow, she is able to pull the pebble out of its side chamber and across the burrow behind her where it forms an effectively impenetrable barrier.

Yet another Australian spider, *Dekana*, digs a U-shaped burrow, with a side chamber at the bottom of the U. One entrance is kept permanently open while the other is loosely covered with debris. Should an enemy enter the main entrance, the spider makes good her escape through the hidden one.

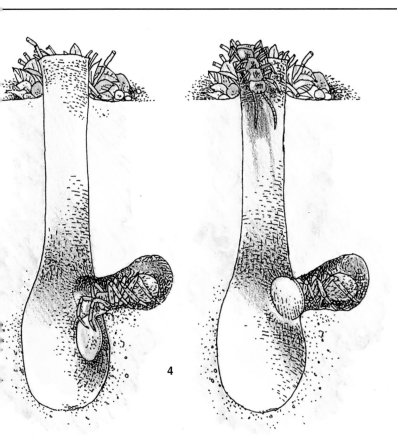

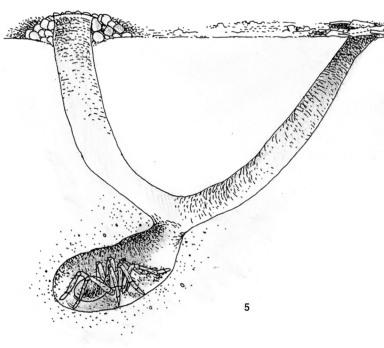

4 When *Lampropodus iridescens* from Australia is threatened, it retreats into a side-shaft off the main burrow and pulls a trap door shut behind it

5 *Dekana* is an Australian mygalomorph that digs a side chamber off the main burrow and loosely caps it with debris. If threatened, it can then rush up its escape route to safety, pushing through the debris with ease.

ACTIVE DEFENSE

Spiders are in the main very small creatures when compared with their enemies, and consequently they usually cut and run when threatened in any way. The fast-moving daylight hunters will do this literally, some of them showing quite a turn of speed as they head for the nearest safe haven. Web-builders are somewhat more exposed, and those which have a lair will often retreat into this when danger threatens. Alternatively, they just drop off the web, with their dragline running behind them so that they can return to the web once the danger is past. These particular spiders usually feign death for a while, and the author has found this to be true of some of the nocturnal hunters if they are accidentally disturbed from their lairs during the day.

If all else fails and a spider is threatened by a predator, it will often adopt a defensive posture in which it makes itself look as large and intimidating as possible. This behavior is very characteristic of the mygalomorphs, and this example (right) of a male

Australian trap-door spider shows how formidable they can appear. The same can be said for the large female sparassid (below), maintaining a defensive posture inside her nest of leaves in Malaysia.

SPIDERS THAT STAND THEIR GROUND

There are some spiders which, if unable to make good their escape, are able to act aggressively toward an enemy. One such is the daddy longlegs spider *Pholcus*, which has evolved an interesting behavior pattern which it uses both in defense and offense. It involves the spider standing out away from its web on its very long legs and rapidly whirling its body in a circle, its legs remaining firmly anchored on the silk. In its own web, this behavior deters other spiders such as *Portia* species, which feed on *Pholcus*. Enemies of *Pholcus* include a number of different species of *Portia*, and it has been discovered that the most effective are those who are better able to avoid setting off the whirling defense behavior. In laboratory tests, it was also found that this whirling of the body deterred the rightful owner from attacking when *Pholcus* entered its web.

Some of the mygalomorphs are covered in a dense pelt of fine hairs, and if these are examined under the microscope they turn out to be both very sharp and barbed with tiny hooks. If a vertebrate predator threatens the spider, it raises its abdomen and vibrates its hind legs against it to release a cloud of these stinging hairs. The effect of these upon the delicate membranes of the nose and eyes of the predator is quite devastating, and the spider can make good its escape. Some South American tree-dwelling mygalomorphs use an alternative defense when disturbed. They just turn their rear end toward the attacker and shoot a jet of clear liquid into its face.

Finally, under active defense there is a recently discovered example in one of the true spiders, the American green lynx spider *Peucetia viridans*. The female reaches about 0.75 in (18 mm) in length, so she is not really a big spider. Yet she can point her fangs forward toward an attacker and shoot out a jet of stinging venom a distance of up to 8 in (200 mm), or over 10 times her own body length.

SWIMMING TO SAFETY

Spiders which live on or around water have an escape route, for when they are threatened a number of them are able to dive below the surface to escape. This is certainly true of *Dolomedes*, the swamp or fishing spider, and the lycosids of the genus *Pirata*, for the water surface is their natural hunting ground. There are, however, a number of species which retreat below the surface as a last resort, though they live on vegetation above rather than on the surface of the water. One such is the orb-web spider *Acanthepeira venusta* from the southeastern states. If disturbed, it either drops down or walks down a plant stem into the water, where it can remain submerged for up to three minutes. The pisaurid *Trechelea manauensis* lives in the inundation forests of Brazil, and it exhibits two interesting escape mechanisms relating to its watery environment. During the wet season, the base of the tree on whose surface it lives is submerged. At this time the spider, if threatened, will run down the trunk and enter the water, remaining on the bark below the surface for up to 15 minutes. Alternatively, the spider is able to make good its escape by running across the surface of the water to another tree. Most spiders, however, if they fall into water have little chance of survival.

The green lynx spider Peucetia viridians *from tropical and subtropical Amercia has been reported as having the ability to spit poison as a defense. We do not know, however, whether the female standing guard over her offspring (left) in Costa Rico would use this capability in their defense.*

CAMOUFLAGE

You might think that spiders are camouflaged both to hide from their prey as it approaches, and to hide from predators. The truth of the matter is that it is only the second case that counts, for the arthropods which form the major prey of spiders are unable to appreciate that a spider is camouflaged. The spiders themselves make use of camouflage in two ways.

CRYPTIC COLORATION

In the first instance, they may have cryptic coloration, that is, their color matches that of their background. A simple example is that of the green spiders from a number of different families, which spend their lives hunting on the green leaves of the plants upon which they dwell. Crypsis only works for an animal, however, if it is accompanied by certain behavioral adaptations. A cryptic spider is only going to be successful as long as it remains still; once it moves, it will be immediately visible to a predator. The spiders therefore have two possible answers to this problem: either they remain absolutely motionless during daylight hours and are active at night, or they move very slowly and stealthily during the day.

This said, there are some notable exceptions to the rule, especially in fast-moving hunting spiders. One example is that of the little lycosid wolf spider, *Arctosa perita*, which the author has seen many times running around on sand dunes along the coastline of the British Isles. This spider has a mottled coloration much like the sand on which it lives. When disturbed, it moves very rapidly across the sand for a short distance, then stops dead and just vanishes. It is actually still there, but it blends in so well with the background that it becomes invisible. Only a close examination of the area of sand where it was last seen will eventually reveal it, although by then it might be on the run again, only to disappear once more the next time it stops. The American *A. littoralis* is a very similar spider and lives in the same sort of sandy environment.

One other habitat which is occupied by camouflaged spiders is the bark of trees. In many cases, tree bark is covered in lichens, algae, mold and mosses, and the spider's markings match these precisely. Once again, the rule is keep still or be seen, but additionally, many bark-dwelling species are flattened so that they create the minimum amount of shadow, which would otherwise make them stand out.

Crypsis is only of real importance to spiders that habitually sit out in the open, and the crab spiders fit well into this category. A number of these from around the world routinely sit and ambush their prey on flowers and thus are referred to as flower spiders. One such spider which, because it is quite common both in the U.S.A. and Europe, has attracted much attention from arachnologists is *Misumena vatia*. The author knows this spider quite well, for it occasionally turns up in his backyard and is common on flowers along an old railroad trackbed close to his home. *M. vatia* is most commonly pure white in color, sometimes with red striping on the side of the abdomen.

In this state it spends much of its time on white or at least very pale-colored flowers. By remaining motionless, it appears to the untrained eye to be just part of the flower. It also has the ability to change color to a bright buttercup yellow, when as often as not it sits on bright-yellow flowers. What is so interesting, however, is that in this form it may also

sit on, for example, a blue flower where to us it sticks out like a sore thumb.

So how does it get away with this apparently careless behavior? The answer is quite simple: the major danger in its exposed position is attack by birds, and birds are rather stupid. Even if they can see the spider's color, which in many cases they cannot, they do not realize that a blue flower does not often have a yellow center, so they just ignore it. And as long as the spider stays still it is safe.

BLENDING IN WITH THE SURROUNDINGS

The second example of spiders using camouflage is when they contrive to make their lairs or egg sacs blend in with the surroundings. Here, of course, there are no problems of movement. It is just a case of the spider incorporating suitable materials from its surroundings into the silk which makes up the lair or egg sac. Apart from such local materials, spiders also add the remains of their arthropod food to the outside of their lairs so that they resemble a pile of trash.

Camouflage, that is, matching color and pattern to fit in with the background, is an art that reaches its zenith in spiders such as the lichen spider Pandercetes gracilis *(opposite) from Australia. This female is sitting with her legs and body pressed hard against the trunk of the tree on which she habitually lives. Her markings and the tufts of hairs on her legs cleverly mimic the lichens encrusting the bark. Just below her head is her egg sac, also camouflaged with a peppering of debris taken from the surface of the bark. A photograph does not do justice to the way in which the egg mass of the possible* Clitaetra *species (above left) blends into the silvery background of the bark on which it has been laid. In this instance, the female normally sits camouflaged against her egg mass rather than sitting on the bark. Tropical lynx spiders of the genus* Peucetia *such as P.* madagascariensis *(below left) from Madagascar are active hunters among vegetation, and as a result many of them are green.*

MIMICRY

Whereas camouflage involves matching one's colors to one's background, a mimic copies the shape of some other object, animate or inanimate, within its environment, and there are spiders which come into both categories. In mimicking an inanimate object, it is important to choose one that is not in itself edible – leaves, buds, twigs or bird droppings.

The last object, on account of its shape, that you might expect a spider to mimic is a leaf, but a number do. Most resemble dead, curled-up leaves, shapes which can be accommodated within the body form of the average spider. The scorpion spider of the genus *Arachnura* from Australasia has an elongated abdomen with two small protuberances on the tip of the dorsal surface. When disturbed, it curls the elongated part of the abdomen over its back in the manner of a scorpion. As often as not, however, it hangs head down in its web, the elongated abdomen resembling the stalk and the body and pulled-in legs the curled-up blade of a dead leaf.

Throughout the neotropical region (South and Central America and the Caribbean) are found the crab spiders of the genus *Onocolus*. They pull their legs into the sides of their body to make themselves appear broader than they actually are, and the tip of the abdomen has a slim extension so that they resemble a small, dead leaf which has fallen out of the canopy onto a leaf in the lower shrub and herb layer of the forest. This allows them to sit out on a leaf in the open with little danger from searching predators. One of the best leaf mimics of all, however, lives in

Some of the more attractive crab spiders spend much of their time sitting in flowers waiting to capture visiting insects. Misumena vatia (left), which is found in both Europe and the U.S.A., is normally white. However, it has the ability to change its color to yellow, the process taking about 24 hours. Even prettier, and much more difficult to find because of its effective camouflage, is the female of Thomisus onustus (above) from Europe, here sitting on the flowering head of a spotted orchid.

IMITATION BIRD DROPPINGS

One speciality is that of mimicking bird droppings, which are not desirable objects as food for anything but butterflies, who imbibe the water and salts that they contain. These spiders tend to be colored in contrasting dark browns and blacks and white, and may also be very shiny so that they appear to glisten. One species of crab spider, *Phrynarachne decipiens* from New Guinea, not only has the right coloration, but it also places little white "splashes" of silk around it on the leaf where it sits, giving the impression of a dropping which has gone "splat" onto the leaf.

Leaf mimicry is not easy for a spider since their shapes do not exactly match. The nearest that spiders can get is a dry, crinkled leaf, well illustrated by the araneid Caerostris sexcuspidata *(right), seen here in the South*

African rainforest. It is, however, much easier for spiders to mimic bird droppings. Phyrarachne rugosa *(below) from Madagascar, for example, resembles the droppings of a fruit-eating bird.*

Spiders, such as the unidentified species (left) from the fast-disappearing Atlantic-coast rainforest of Brazil, sometimes mimic a dead leaf just lying around on living leaves in the forest. Other species, however, adopt a different strategy by hanging from a length of silk, so that they resemble a leaf still on the tree. The female Micrathena *(below left) is doing just this in a rainforest in Mexico, while* Arachnura scorpionoides *(opposite) from Madagascar has gone one step farther. Her long, slim abdomen resembles a leaf stalk, and her body the rolled-up leaf blade, as she hangs below her egg sac. Although a human sees fairly easily through the disguise of the Australian* Poltys *(below), to a foraging bird it probably seems to be merely an inedible bud protruding from the twig.*

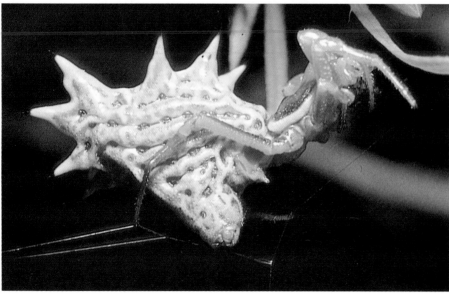

the lower layers of the humid tropical forests of Madagascar. *Augusta glyphica* is an araneid found only on this island, and it is related to the widespread *Gasteracantha species*, characterized by their flattened bodies and peculiar, pointed abdominal outgrowths. *Augusta* is flattened in the extreme and with its broad body, brown coloration and habit of hanging in its web, looks for all the world like a dead leaf.

With the net-throwing spiders having common names like stick spiders because of their shape, and the slim-bodied tetragnathids being called grass spiders, it is clear that they do mimic other objects.

ANT MIMICRY

Spiders from a number of different families are mimics of ants, though this may seem an odd thing for them to do. The reasons, however, are twofold. In the first instance, ants have painful bites and this deters some animals from attempting to eat them. A spider which is a good ant mimic will also be afforded this protection. In the second place, a spider which looks similar enough to an ant is likely to be accepted by it so that the spider can get close enough to catch it. In most ant-mimicking spiders, not only does the appearance of the spider resemble that of an ant, for example the spider's abdomen may carry striped markings to match the segmentation of the ant's abdomen, but its behavior does also. These spiders tend to walk in an antlike, zigzag fashion and they often raise the front pair of legs and wave them about like a pair of antennae. Some ant-mimicking spiders live in close association with their ant models, while others live a solitary life in a habitat occupied by the ants.

Jumping spiders of the genus *Myrmarachne* appear to be examples of ant mimics which leave their models alone, for they have not been observed to feed on ants. Several species living within a relatively small area in Ghana have been studied in detail, and it turns out that each particular spider tends to be associated with only a single species of ant. Since they associate with ants but do not feed on them, we must assume that they gain protection from their resemblance to the ants. It has been observed that the ants will actually attack unspecialized predatory birds, though they have no protection against ant specialists such as woodpeckers or certain lizards. Under attack from the latter, *Myrmarachne* does not behave like an ant, but instead runs away and hides. If the attack persists, the spider will eventually drop to safety on its dragline.

In order to live safely with its ant models, *Myrmarachne* has had to adapt its behavior, for the former are quite formidable adversaries when roused. Whereas some ant-mimicking spiders are readily accepted by their hosts, *Myrmarachne* is not. If it gets too close, the spider elicits an aggressive response from the ants. As it is a jumping spider with good eyesight, however, it is able to avoid the ants' aggression, either by hiding or jumping out of reach. Should it fail to escape, the spider is killed and eaten.

One time at which the spider is very vulnerable to ant attack is during mating, when the pair are unable to leap to safety. To overcome this problem, the spider has evolved the strategy of mating in a silk retreat built by the female. The eggs are then laid in the retreat, where they are also protected from ant attack.

The ant-mimicking *Strophius nigricans* (family *Thomisidae*) and *Aphantochilus sp.* (family *Aphantochilidae*) both feed upon ants, which are usually captured by attacking them from behind. Once the ants are caught, the spiders attempt to hold their legs away from the ground until

The unidentified ant-mimicking salticid spider (right) comes from the same general area as the mimicry pairs in the diagram below. It bustles around the forest floor in a manner very typical of an ant. Cosmophasis *from Kenya (opposite) is a jumping spider that mimics ants so that it can approach them without being attacked. The spider in the photograph is in the act of immobilizing a type of ant that forms its main prey.*

the poison takes effect, as well as keeping well clear of the ant's jaws. Both types of spider use the corpse of the ant as a shield if they are subsequently approached by patroling ants of the same species. If this fails to deter the ants, then the spiders, being faster movers than the ants, just run away from them. Since ants are potentially dangerous adversaries, at least one spider has evolved the strategy of hiding during the day and only hunting its prey at night, when ant colonies are relatively inactive. The ants on which the zodariid *Zodarium frenatum* feeds leave a single guard outside the nest at night, and it is this luckless individual that usually falls prey to the spider.

ANT-MIMICKING SPIDERS

All of the ants and spiders shown here were collected in the same area of rainforest in Brazil. They are arranged in mimicry pairs of spider and ant. To the untrained eye it may be difficult to distinguish between them, but all of the ants have a pair of antennae on the front of their heads and their abdomens show clear segmentation.

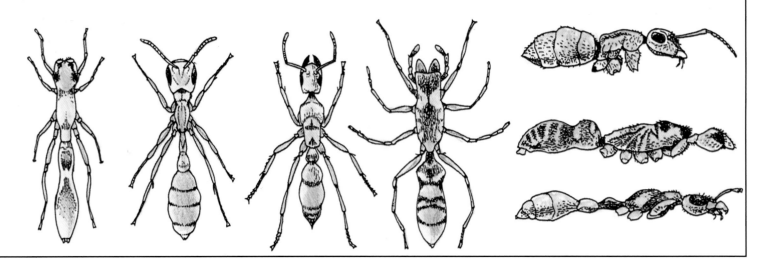

WASP MIMICS

Whereas many harmless insects gain protection by mimicking other unpleasant species such as wasps, this type of mimicry is absent in spiders because they do not fly. There is, however, an exception, for among the wasps is a family, the *Mutillidae*, characterized by their wingless females and their exceedingly painful sting. This winglessness coupled with the sting has allowed the evolution of a number of spider mimics in tropical regions of the world.

The jumping spider (right) is possibly a mimic of the mutillid wasp (below), for both have similar markings and they live together in the same area of rainforest in Brazil.

BACK-TO-FRONT MIMICS

Although the few known mutillid-mimicking spiders are orientated the same way as their models, that is, the head end of the spider is the head end of the model, at least one species does things back to front. The spider in question is *Orsima formica*, a remarkable 0.25-in- (6-mm)-long jumping spider from Borneo. The abdomen is separated into two regions by a narrow waist, so that the hindmost section represents the head of the wasp model, the foremost section the thorax, and the cephalothorax the model's abdomen. The species has unusually long spinnerets for a salticid, one pair

mimicking a pair of antennae and the other a pair of jaws. These are dark in color, as are the hind legs, making the latter stand out as the forelegs of the model, since the other pairs of legs are pale in comparison. Apart from its overall insect appearance, the spider has also modified its behavior to resemble that of a mutillid wasp. It often stands with the abdomen raised so that the false "head" is apparent. The head effect is enhanced by the movement of the spinnerets mimicking the antennae. At intervals, the abdomen is lowered to bring the jaw-mimicking spinnerets into

contact with the surface upon which the spider is standing, giving the effect of feeding, especially when these spinnerets are moved from side to side in the manner of insect jaws. It would appear that if indeed this spider resembles a mutillid wasp to potential predators, then it derives its protection from Batesian mimicry, that is, mimicking something distasteful when you actually are not. Its behavior, however, also provides it with a means of escape, for if a predator goes for the model "head," it will retreat backward in the opposite direction to that expected as the spider runs away.

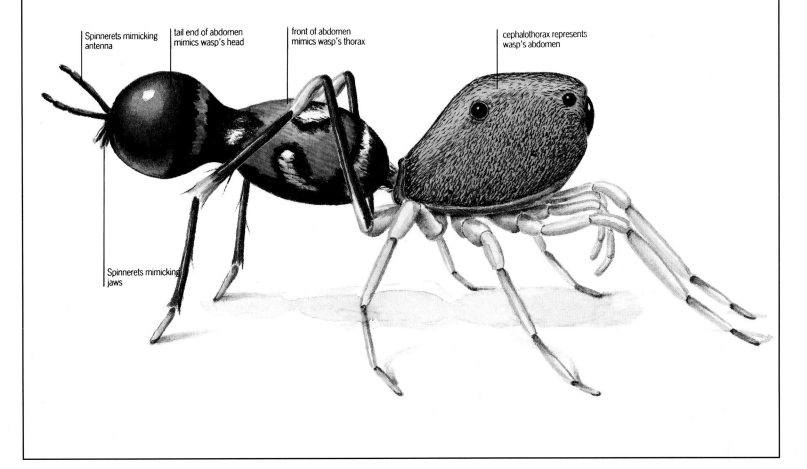

Spinnerets mimicking antenna

tail end of abdomen mimics wasp's head

front of abdomen mimics wasp's thorax

cephalothorax represents wasp's abdomen

Spinnerets mimicking jaws

TROPICAL FOREST SPIDERS

The world's tropical forests contain a greater diversity of life than any other habitat, and in consequence they are the home of a multitude of spider species from many different families. Illustrated here are some of the spiders that might be found in the tropical forests of South America. Colorful jumping spiders (**1**) are a feature of this type of habitat from southern Mexico to northern Argentina, and whenever they jump on their prey they always trail a lifeline of silk behind them. The two-tailed spiders (**2**) of the family *Hersiliidae* tend to be found in the less dense parts of the forest, such as along highways or around the edges of clearings, where they may be found pressed hard against tree bark in a highly camouflaged pose. Ctenoid wandering spiders such as *Cupiennius* (**3**) hunt actively on foliage at night for insects and other prey, but during daylight hours they lie stretched out along a leaf or stem. Not all is what it seems in the tropical forest, for what looks like an ant (**4**) may in reality be the clubionid spider *Myrmecium*. As in most habitats with plenty of supports, these forests abound in orb-web spiders, though they do not like the gloomiest areas of dense forest. The silver orb-weaver *Argiope argentata* (**5**) is one such spider. It has a very wide distribution since it is found not only in South and Central America, but also extends into the U.S.A.

SCALE

1 Jumping spider, ³⁄₁₆ in (5mm).
2 Two-tailed spider, ⅞ in (12mm).
3 *Cupiennius,* 1in (25mm).
4 *Myrmecium,* ³⁄₁₆ in (5mm).
5 *Argiope argentata,* ⁹⁄₁₆ in (15mm).

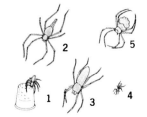

ENEMIES OF SPIDERS

Despite the fact that spiders are generally formidable predators, they themselves have a large number of enemies that either feed directly on them or are parasites upon them. Spiders are, of course, relatively soft-bodied and as such form an important source of food for many small birds and insectivorous mammals, as well as reptiles such as lizards and amphibians such as frogs and toads. In Australia, for example, apart from vertebrate predators such as bandicoots, which dig mygalomorph spiders

SPIDER-EATERS

Just how much effect a predator can have on spider numbers in a particular habitat was shown in a long-term field experiment carried out in the Bahamas. During this investigation, when lizards were excluded from the experimental plots, there were three times as many spiders recorded as when the lizards were present, so they were having a profound effect on spider numbers under natural conditions. When the diet of the lizards was analyzed, it was found that they ate both spiders and also insects that the spiders preyed on.

Spiders have numerous enemies. Perhaps the most obvious are birds, such as the European great tit Parus major (above) and its cousins the chickadees in the U.S.A. In the tropical rainforest of Madagascar the day gecko Phelsuma quadriocellata (left) will also take its toll of spiders, as will the Central American squirrel monkey Saimiri oerstedii (opposite, bottom). As they forage, these and other species of monkey ransack the forest, turning over leaves, pulling off loose bark, and investigating every nook and cranny, so that even for the most cryptic of spiders there may be no hiding place.

out of their burrows, their main enemies are other arthropods. Both centipedes and various species of scorpions have been recorded as entering burrows of and feeding upon a whole range of these subterranean spiders, and this is no doubt true for the other parts of the world where such spiders are to be found.

SPIDER-HUNTING WASPS

Vertebrate predators, scorpions and centipedes are perhaps the more obvious of the spider's enemies, but there are other, more insidious creatures who make a habit of preying upon spiders. Most notable of these are the spider-hunting wasps. They have a worldwide distribution and among the most spectacular of them are members of the genus *Pepsis* from the U.S.A. They are large, metallic-bluish or -greenish wasps with rust-colored wings that may attain a span of up to 4 in (100 mm). They hunt mygalomorph tarantulas, each species of wasp requiring a particular species of spider for its prey. If, for example, a wasp is confined in a cage with the wrong species of spider, the wasp will ignore it, and during the night is likely to be killed when the spider becomes active. They have a strict preference for the female spiders, which are bulkier and therefore contain a greater supply of food for the wasp's young.

In order to decide whether or not it has found the correct spider, the wasp must actually contact it with her antenna. The spider allows her actually to crawl under it and walk over it during the inspection without showing any hostile response. The wasp, having decided that the spider is of the correct species, then walks away a short distance to dig the burrow which will be the latter's grave. Despite their own powerful jaws,

Anoplius infuscatus (above) from Europe is one of a number of specialist wasp species from various parts of the world that provision their nests with the paralyzed corpses of spiders.

the spiders put up no defense against the wasp once it confronts them, and the wasp finds no difficulty in stinging the spider. She then waits until the venom has taken effect and paralyzed the spider before she drags it to her burrow. Once the spider is safely cached, the female wasp lays a single egg on it and then seals the burrow up. The wasp grub which hatches from the egg is thus guaranteed a supply of fresh food from the paralyzed spider. It is not known why the spiders behave in such a passive way with the wasp. *Pepsis* is known to produce a pungent odor when excited, and maybe this in some way pacifies the spider.

Whereas a single large female mygalomorph is sufficient food for a single *Pepsis* grub, wasps which catch smaller spiders may have to provision their burrows with several in order to supply enough food for their developing offspring. Also, whereas many spider-hunting wasps dig burrows in the soil, some have a more specialized way of doing things. Important enemies of spiders in warm countries are the mud-dauber wasps of the genus *Sceliphron*. These wasps construct mud tubes which they provision with spiders to feed their solitary larva. Tubes of the wasp *S. spirifex* in Malawi contained an average of 15 spiders from more than eight different families, mostly captured from the trees and shrubs of its surroundings. A common spider which was interestingly absent was *Myrmarachne*, an ant-mimicking species, which may provide evidence that such mimicry protects spiders from hunting wasps.

At least one spider-hunting wasp has been seen to make use of one of the spider's natural responses in order to facilitate the latter's capture. This particular wasp, *Pison morosum*, bumps purposefully into the web of its main prey, the theridiid *Achaeranea verculata*. This triggers off the spider's escape response, where it drops out of its web on its dragline, in this instance to be immediately picked off by the waiting wasp. In Sardinia, the wasp *Anoplius sardus* specializes in trap-door mygalomorphs of the genus *Nemesia*. The wasp attempts to coax the spider out of its burrow by lifting the trap door, but if it is unsuccessful, it will actually dig down into the burrow behind the spider and capture it in this manner.

MANTISPIDS

Within the insect order *Neuroptera* is a family whose larvae specialize in developing spiders as a source of food. Members of the *Mantispidae* have front legs that are adapted for catching prey, similar to those of the

ATTACKING THE EGG SAC

It is possible within the suborder *Mantispinae* to recognize three categories of individual insect from their behavior.
1 Obligate penetrators have to find an egg sac once it has been produced before they can enter it.
2 Obligate spider-boarders have to ride on the female spider before they can enter the egg sac.
3 Facultative spider-boarders can find an egg sac either directly or via a ride on the female spider.

When they are able to, spiders will make an attempt to escape from their enemies, and the wolf spider Pirata piraticus (above) from Europe is no exception. When threatened, it will dive below the surface of the pond on and around which it hunts. It is more difficult to escape the attentions of the mantispid Climaciella (left). This example is from Brazil and is a wasp mimic. The larvae feed on the spiderlings as they develop inside the egg sac, so they have no defense other than the ability of the female spider to hide the egg sac in the first place.

praying mantids, and it is this characteristic which gives the family its name. The female mantispid lays her eggs on the surface of a leaf or some other convenient structure, and the larvae which hatch from them can gain access to the spider egg sac in one of two ways. Either the matispid larva finds an egg sac and penetrates it or else it finds a female spider and sits on her until she lays her eggs; the larva then enters the spider's egg sac as it is produced.

A most interesting discovery has recently been made about the larvae of *Mantispa uhleri* from North America. Since mantispid larvae feed directly upon the eggs and developing young of the spider, they are predators rather than parasites, but the larva of *M. uhleri* also has the facility to be a true parasite. If the larva finds an immature female spider, then instead of leaving her for a mature female, it remains and feeds upon the spider's body fluids until such a time as she matures and lays her eggs.

OTHER PREDATORS

Spiders have also to face up to a number of other arthropod enemies. Some of the parasitic wasps and flies lay their eggs upon the spider, and the larva which hatches then feeds upon the living spider, getting gradually larger as the spider slowly shrinks. When the parasites are fully grown, the spider dies. In Central America, at least one species of damselfly plucks orb-web spiders from the center of their webs and eats them, and blood-sucking sandflies have been seen to feed upon large *Nephila* females. A number of spiders have been found carrying mites on their surface. Some of these have turned out to be true parasites, feeding upon the spider's body fluids; others exhibit phoresis, that is, they live on the spider and feed upon various waste products associated with the host's lifestyle.

One group of living organisms are so abundant in soil and plants that it has been said that if everything but them was taken away and the earth was viewed from space its outline would still be visible. The organisms in question are the roundworms. Although many are free-living, many are parasites and they include spiders among their hosts. The family *Mermithidae* in particular are parasites of arthropods, and one species can become a pest in locusts kept in laboratories for research. Spiders pick up the worm in larval form from their insect prey, with the insect acting as an intermediate host. The worm then feeds and grows in the spider's abdomen until the host eventually dies and the worm is released into the soil, where it lays its eggs. These are then ingested by an insect and the life cycle is repeated. These worms have been recorded as attaining lengths 20 times that of the host. In human terms, this would be equivalent to harboring a worm over 100 ft (31 m) in length.

DIVING WASPS

A most amazing hunting wasp is *Anoplius depressipes* from North America, for she specializes in catching the fishing spider *Dolomedes triton* as her prey. She normally hunts this spider on the water surface, where it tends to hide from the wasp among the leaves of the water plants growing there. If, as she can, *Dolomedes* dives below the water surface to escape the wasp's attention, the wasp will also dive below the surface and swim down, using its wings, to sting and paralyze the spider underwater. The wasp then brings her prey out of the water and takes it to her burrow.

Among the most unpleasant of the spiders' enemies are the parasitic wasps, for their depredations lead to a lingering death. The wasp lays an egg on the surface of the spider, and when the wasp grub hatches it begins slowly to consume its host's internal organs, while its body, which remains outside the spider (below), gets ever larger. Eventually the wasp larva drops off and pupates, and the luckless spider dies.

CONSERVATION OF SPIDERS

The conservation of spiders depends on the conservation of their habitats. Before looking at that, however, there is one important point to make in connection with keeping spiders as pets.

SPIDERS AS PETS

In recent years, the keeping of furry mygalomorph tarantulas as pets has become quite popular. Unfortunately in the early days these spiders all came from the wild, and as a consequence the most popular of these, the Mexican red-kneed *Brachypelma smithi*, was overcollected. This spider has now been added to C.I.T.E.S. (Convention on International Trade in Endangered Species) Appendix II so that a permit will now have to be issued by Mexico for each spider it wishes to export to a C.I.T.E.S.-observing country.

If you wish to keep to one of these spiders, please try and buy one that you are sure has been bred in captivity, for a number of dealers are now successfully doing so. If there is no demand for these creatures, then nobody will bother to capture them and they will not become endangered, as has happened with so many other animals, such as parrots and monkeys.

CONSERVING THE SPIDER'S HABITAT

In so far as direct action to conserve spiders is concerned, the author is aware of only one attempt to do so, and that is in England. The swamp spider *Dolomedes plantarius* is known in the British Isles in just one wetland locality in Suffolk, though it is not uncommon in the rest of Europe. As a consequence of the general lowering of the water table in the area, money was actually spent on improving the habitat for the spider, which requires open water to survive.

Conservation of spiders in the wild means, of course, setting aside where necessary nature reserves and suitable areas of land protected under the law. Everyone is aware of the alarming rate at which, for example, the world's rainforests are disappearing. With them go many animals and plants, including some spiders which have probably not yet even been described, for as yet we perhaps know of less than half of the world's spider species. Many people become upset about what is happening to the rainforests without realizing that equally terrible things are taking place on our own doorsteps.

How can you attempt to stop such things from happening? The simple answer is to become a member of local conservation bodies, countrywide conservation bodies, and learned societies such as the American or British Arachnological societies. In this way, individual voices can be joined in a chorus of "No" each time we see an irreplaceable part of our heritage about to disappear under the chainsaw and the bulldozer.

SPIDERS AND MAN

The ambivalent feeling that many people have toward spiders no doubt stems from the conflict as to whether they are "good" or "bad." Leaving aside the fact that a certain number of them are venomous, they have both advantages and disadvantages as far as humans are concerned. The webs that they build and the draglines they leave behind are very long-lived, since the silk is coated with a layer of antibiotic which wards off normal bacterial and fungal decay. These enduring remains of the spiders' toils are the bane of the life of the average houseowner, forming as they do untidy cobwebs. On the other hand, if it were not for the spiders' cobwebs, our lives would be even further blighted by those most hateful of pests, the disease-ridden housefly and the cockroach.

THE ALTERNATIVE PEST-CONTROLLER

Looking at the subject of "good" spiders more seriously, it is only in recent times that we have come to realize the important role that spiders play in the control of serious insect pests. The present way of controling these, at least in the wealthier, developed countries, is by the use of a great range of pesticides, with their accompanying disadvantages. As people become more concerned about the dangers of the wholesale use of chemicals, is there any evidence that spiders could provide a natural form of pest control? From the results produced by an increasing number of researchers looking at this subject, the answer seems to be yes, up to a point.

It has been found that in rice fields in California the wolf spider *Pardosa ramulosa* is an important predator of the aster leafhopper. This insect is a rice pest, and experiments have shown that, if up to 22 spiders/sq yd are introduced to the fields, the pest is reduced in density by between 84 and 96 percent. Spiders have also been found to be important in controling the numbers of two other species of plant-bug pests in Asian ricefields. In China, for example, it has been found that the number of offspring produced by wolf spiders in paddyfields increases as the numbers of the plant-hoppers, a bug pest, increases. On a different crop, corn, it was found in Texas that spiders were a major predator of the southwest cornborer, the larva of a pyralid moth. It is to be hoped that this sort of information will result in less blanket use of insecticides in the future and a greater use of biological control by spiders and other creatures, to everyone's benefit.

It has become fashionable in recent years to be the proud owner of one of the large, hairy mygalomorph spiders. One of the most popular of these has been the Mexican red-kneed spider, but individuals of the genus Pamphoboetus, *such as the example photographed in semidesert in Chile (left), are also kept as pets.*

SOME TIPS ON CONSERVING SPIDERS

1 Do not wash house spiders down the bathtub drain. They did not get into the tub that way, an old-wives tale, but are wandering males (in search of females) who have fallen in and cannot climb out up the smooth side of the bath.

2 Do not be obsessively neat in the yard. Leave somewhere for spiders to build their lairs. Piles of stones, bricks, tiles or logs hidden away in a corner will attract many species. Numerous linyphiid spiders live in leaf litter, especially during the winter, so do not sweep up all the leaves in the fall. Plant as many trees and shrubs as possible as these will attract spiders, and leave a corner of the yard completely wild where spiders and other creatures can exist with the minimum of disturbance.

3 Do not use insecticide sprays indiscriminately, for they are often just as good at killing spiders and other useful insects as they are at killing pests.

4 When you search for spiders under stones, logs, etc., please remember to replace them exactly as you found them.

5 Become a member of your local nature-conservation group. Your membership dues will help them to set up nature reserves that will aid in the conservation of many spider species. Since these reserves are often in threatened habitats, they may be important in conserving some of the rarer species.

OBSERVATION OF SPIDERS

From time to time, cases occur of people in Britain being fined for failing to look after a pet spider properly, on the basis that "spiders too have feelings." Whether this is true or not is conjectural, but spiders should always be treated with care and compassion, as should all creatures unless they are a direct threat to our safety. This should be borne in mind when handling them for examination or looking at them in the wild.

Finding spiders is no real problem. Web-builders may often be found in full view on vegetation or other suitable structures, or they may build sheet webs on the ground. You may also discover them in flowers, on and under leaves, under logs, rocks and stones, in leaf litter, wandering around on the leaves of floating water plants, almost anywhere in fact. Having found your spider, how do you catch it? The answer is, for most spiders, with care, for they are soft-bodied and easily damaged. Larger spiders may be coaxed into a glass or plastic tube or a small, clear plastic box and then examined with a magnifying glass. Smaller spiders have to be sucked up in an aspirator, commonly called a "pooter" (see diagram), and then transferred to a small glass tube for examination, either with a powerful magnifying glass or even better with a binocular microscope. If you have the materials available, it is easier to examine smaller spiders by making the simple but useful viewing-chamber shown in the diagram.

If you intend to take spiders home to look at them, they will need at the very least some damp blotting or filter paper in their container, for although they can survive for weeks without food, they do need a regular supply of moisture. If you do take spiders from the wild, please replace them in the same or a similar habitat.

PHOTOGRAPHING SPIDERS AND THEIR WEBS

One of the challenges which some readers might wish to accept is to take color photographs of spiders. In order to do this, you will need a camera with at least some degree of close-focusing ability and, unless you use a very fast film, some means of illuminating the subject. The ideal equipment, which has been used for all of the photographs in this book, is a single-lens reflex camera with a macro lens. The sun is not a good source of light for closeup photography, so in addition you will need a small flash-gun, one which can be hand-held, not mounted on the camera. Even better if you can afford it is a pair of through-the-lens flash-guns mounted one on each side of the camera. With this combination, the camera reads the amount of light that has fallen on to the subject from the flashes and when this is correct, it quenches them. Thus all exposures are accurate.

With a single flash, hold the camera in the right hand and the flash in the left with the ball of the left thumb against the camera

A SIMPLE SPIDER CAGE

The construction of the cage is simple. The plastic tray with holes in the base should be stood on something like a sheet of wet capillary matting to keep the compost moist. The diameter of the nylon mesh should be small enough to keep the spiders in, and the glass tube should be large enough to drop prey items such as flies through. Twigs could be added for web-building spiders, and stones or bark for those species that like to lurk in dark recesses.

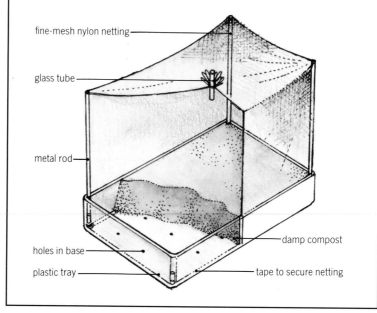

fine-mesh nylon netting

glass tube

metal rod

holes in base

plastic tray

damp compost

tape to secure netting

Although it is just possible to obtain adequate photographs of spiders and other arachnids using natural lighting and fast film, it is essential to use an electronic flash-gun to photograph them at night or in the gloom of a forest.

Since many arachnids are nocturnal, it is worth looking for them by flashlight. The degree of photographic success possible can be seen in the closeup shot of an Isopoda *huntsman spider (above) photographed at night in Australia.*

body to support it. The macro lens will allow you to focus down to 1:1, but beyond this you will need a set of extension tubes and/or lens reversing tubes to take pictures of the smaller spiders. A good book on wildlife photography will give you all of the details.

One aspect of spiders that is well worth photographing is their webs. The best time to do this, if you live in the right sort of climate, is when they are covered in dew or frost and the silk shows up very clearly. If this is not possible where you live, then do the next best thing and spray the web with a very fine mist of water, which will make it appear to be dew-covered.

Photography of spiders' webs is best carried out when they are covered in either dew, like that of Linyphia trianqularis *(left), or when covered in hoarfrost, like*

that of the garden spider Areneus diadematus *(above). Both were in the author's garden.*

FAMILY IDENTIFICATION CHART

Spider identification, even to family level, poses problems for the average reader who might wish to, for a microscope is needed to see many of the characteristics used to separate them. The following table gives the major differences between the spider families that you are most likely to see in the British Isles, the U.S.A. and Australia. Not all of these families are to be found in each country. The term "free-living" is used to describe those spiders that do not weave a permanent web in order to trap their prey.

burrows, from which they emerge to hunt actively for prey; the true bird-eating spiders live and hunt in trees.

MYGALOMORPH FAMILIES

ATYPIDAE
Purse-web spiders. Family typically constructs a silk-lined burrow, with the silk extending above ground as a tube that continues across the surface of the ground or up adjacent trees.

THERAPHOSIDAE
Bird-eating spiders. Spiders covered in a velvety layer of hairs. Some American species also possess stinging hairs. Many live in

CTENIZIDAE
Trap-door spiders. Burrowing spiders, the majority of which close their burrows with a trap door. They characteristically bear a rake of teeth, situated on the basal jaw segment, used for digging the burrow.

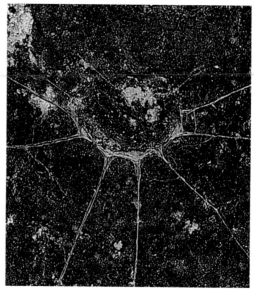

ARANEOMORPH FAMILIES

DICTYNIDAE
Mesh-webbed spiders. Cribellate. Eight eyes. Spiders that include the characteristic hackled bands of cribellum silk in their aerial webs.

AMAUROBIIDAE
Cribellate. Eight eyes. Originally in the *Dictynidae*, they are larger species that build tubular webs containing hackled bands of cribellate silk on the ground, under bark, etc.

DINOPIDAE
Ogre-faced, twig- or net-throwing spiders. Cribellate. Eight eyes. Long, slim-bodied spiders. They weave a web in the form of a net, which is held in the front legs and thrown over prey to capture it.

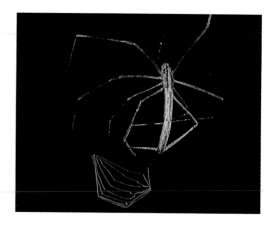

ULOBORIDAE
Cribellate. Eight eyes. They build and catch prey with a horizontal orb-web. Prey is subdued by wrapping it up, since poison glands are absent in this family.

PHOLCIDAE
Daddy-longlegs. Ecribellate. Six or eight eyes. Long-legged spiders with a tubular abdomen. They build a rough aerial sheet-web; prey is wrapped before being bitten.

SCYTODIDAE

Spitting spiders. Ecribellate. Six eyes. Free-living spiders with an enlarged cephalothorax, which contains the modified poison glands for producing gum used for prey capture.

OONOPIDAE

Ecribellate. Six eyes. Minute, free-living, nocturnal hunters that live in silken cells during the day.

DYSDERIDAE

Ecribellate. Six eyes. Free-living nocturnal hunters that spend the day in silken cells under stones, leaf litter, etc. They tend to have noticeably large jaws and a tubular abdomen.

SEGESTRIIDAE

Ecribellate. Six eyes. Slim-bodied spiders that build a tubular lair with traplines.

LOXOSCELIDAE

Violin or brown spiders. Ecribellate. Eight eyes. Generally brown-bodied spiders that are vagrant hunters. Some species are able to bite humans.

CLUBIONIDAE

Ecribellate. Eight eyes. Nocturnal hunters that spend the day hidden in silken cells on vegetation. Distinguished from the similar *Gnaphosidae* by the anterior spinnerets, which are close together and somewhat conical.

GNAPHOSIDAE

Ecribellate. Eight eyes. Nocturnal hunters, usually on the ground, spending the day in a silken cell under stones, etc. Anterior spinnerets well-separated and tubular in shape.

CTENIDAE

Wandering spiders. Ecribellate. Eight eyes. Free-living terrestrial hunters, similar in appearance to the *Lycosidae*. Distinguished from one another by the arrangement of the two rows of eyes, both of which curve backward in the *Ctenidae*, but the front row curves forward in the *Lycosidae*.

THOMISIDAE

Crab spiders. Ecribellate. Eight eyes. Free-living spiders with flattened, somewhat crablike bodies. The first two pairs of legs are longer and stouter than the rest. They sit in exposed situations and ambush passing prey.

PHILODROMIDAE

Ecribellate. Eight eyes. Similar to the *Thomisidae*, but the legs are all similar in length; they tend to hunt more actively.

SPARASSIDAE

Giant crab or huntsman spiders. Ecribellate. Eight eyes, Typically flattened spiders with the legs rotated so that they tend to turn forward. Free-living hunters that live under bark and in cracks in rocks, from which they emerge to seek their prey.

SALTICIDAE

Jumping spiders. Ecribellate. Eight eyes. Active diurnal hunters with large eyes, body often brightly colored. They jump actively from perch to perch while hunting. A few apparently primitive species retain the ability to build a sheet-web and use it as an additional aid for catching prey.

LYCOSIDAE

Wolf spiders. Ecribellate. Eight eyes. Large-eyed hunters. Many are free-living, but a number hunt from the security of their silk-lined burrows. Most often seen running around actively on the ground in many habitats.

PISAURIDAE

Nursery-tent, swamp and fishing spiders. Ecribellate. Eight eyes. Free-living spiders similar to the *Lycosidae*, but whereas the latter hold their egg sacs on the spinnerets, the *Pisauridae* hold them in their jaws.

HERSILIIDAE

Two-tailed spiders. Ecribellate. Eight eyes. Flattened spiders that hunt actively on the surface of trees. They are named for their characteristically elongated posterior pair of spinnerets (in some species they are as long as the abdomen). They often hold these spinnerets vertically away from the body when they run off in alarm.

OXYOPIDAE

Lynx spiders. Ecribellate. Eight eyes. Large-eyed, free-living spiders that hunt actively in daylight, usually on vegetation. Habitats similar to those of jumping spiders, though the oxyopids pounce rather than jump on their prey.

AGELENIDAE

Sheet-web spiders. Ecribellate. Eight eyes. Spiders that typically have a sheet-web extending over adjacent vegetation, rocks, etc, from the entrance of their tubular retreat.

THERIDIIDAE

Comb-footed spiders. Ecribellate. Eight eyes. Spiders with a mainly globular abdomen, which build scaffold-webs of various types. Includes the notorious black widow spiders.

TETRAGNATHIDAE

Grass spiders. Ecribellate. Eight eyes. Often elongated spiders with very large jaws. They catch prey in an orb-web, often inclined at an angle or even horizontal.

ARANEIDAE

Orb-web spiders. Ecribellate. Eight eyes. The typical orb-web builders. Some species incorporate a clearly visible stabilimentum of white silk in the center of the web.

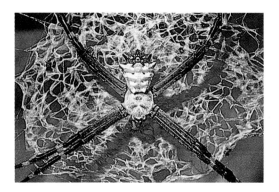

LINYPHIIDAE

Money spiders. Ecribellate. Eight eyes. Mainly from temperate northern regions, these are in general tiny spiders that build sheet-webs among grass and other vegetation. Their sheer abundance can be appreciated by the number of their webs, which are visible in grassy fields on a dewy early fall morning.

GLOSSARY

Appendages A general term to describe any structures, such as legs, palps, jaws or spinnerets, that are attached to the body.

Aggressive mimicry A number of spiders from different families feed upon other spiders by entering their webs and capturing them. The killer attracts its spider prey by shaking the latter's web in the manner of a trapped insect, the so-called aggressive mimicry.

Araneomorphs The true spiders; this includes all spiders other than the mygalomorphs and the primitive *Liphistiidae*.

Ballooning A method of dispersal employed by many young and some smaller adult spiders, in which they are carried around by air currents suspended from a length of silk.

Book lung The structure, consisting of a number of interleaving plates, used by spiders and scorpions to bring about gas exchange between the air and their blood.

Calamistrum A comb of stiff hairs on the metatarsus of the fourth pair of legs of some spiders. It is used to comb out the multistrand silk produced by the cribellum of these spiders.

Carapace The tough shield that covers the upper surface of the cephalothorax in arachnids. It acts as a protection for the delicate internal organs and as an anchor for the muscles of the sucking stomach.

Cephalothorax Structure formed by fusion of the head and thorax and covered on the upper surface by the carapace.

Chelicerae Scientific name for the jaws of arachnids. Each half of the jaw consists of a basal segment upon which hinges the sharp, piercing fang that injects the poison.

Cribellate Possessing a cribellum, as in the spider families *Amaurobiidae, Acanthoctenidae, Dictynidae, Dinopidae, Decobiidae, Tengelidae,* and *Uloboridae*.

Cribellum A special plate through which multistranded silk is secreted. It is derived from a pair of modified spinnerets.

Crypsis Having a coloration that blends into the background, often just referred to as camouflage coloration.

Cuticle The tough body covering forming the exoskeleton, which is typical of all arthropod groups.

Dragline A line of silk that spiders always trail behind them as they move around. It is quite important for free-living spiders as it allows the males to follow and find the females.

Ecdysis Another name for molting.

Ecribellate Describes spiders lacking a cribellum and possessing just the normal spinnerets.

Epigyne Structure at the entrance to the female reproductive opening of spiders. Each species has a structure unique to itself, and these structures are therefore of importance in identifying spider species.

Exoskeleton The external supporting skeleton of arthropods, made of tubes and plates which protect the delicate internal organs and to which the body musculature is attached internally.

Hackled band A special fluffy silk produced by the cribellate spiders, which is extruded by the cribellum and combed out by the calamistrum.

Mimicry The act by which a spider copies the shape of something else, for example, another animal or an inanimate object such as a dead leaf.

Mygalomorphs A term used to describe members of the spider suborder *Mygalomorphae*, which includes the "tarantulas," bird-eating spiders, trap-door and purse-web spiders.

Opisthosoma Another name for the cephalothorax in spiders.

Palpal organ The modified terminal segment of the male spider's pedipalp, which is used to introduce semen into the female's spermathecae during mating.

Pectines Structures on the underside of the scorpion used as mechanoreceptors to test the nature of the ground over which it is moving.

Pedicel The slim waist between the cephalothorax and abdomen of a spider, through which run the various organ systems such as the gut and nerve cord.

Pedipalps A pair of appendages on arachnids on the segment in front of the walking legs often referred to in the text simply as "palps." They are employed as sense organs, but in the male spider the terminal segment is modified to form the palpal organ.

Pheromones Chemical messenges that are transported by air currents, or on the surface of water, from one spider to another, or are attached to the female spider's silk; i.e., sexual scents.

Retina The layer of light-sensitive cells within the eye, which transmit sight information to the brain.

Semen The liquid containing the male sperm, which is introduced into the female's spermathecae via the epigyne.

Sperm web A tiny web constructed by male spiders, onto which they deposit a drop of semen from their reproductive opening on the abdomen. This semen is then taken up into the palpal organ prior to mating.

Spermathecae Sacs in the female which store the male's semen after mating, often for a considerable length of time, until it is required for fertilization of the eggs.

Spermatophore A special capsule deposited by some male arachnids, which contains the semen.

Spiderling The name normally applied to a baby spider just after hatching.

Spinnerets Appendages on the tip of the spider's abdomen from which the various kinds of silk used by spiders are extruded.

Stabilimentum Lines of silk in the web of some orb-web spiders, which reflect ultraviolet light. These lines of silk, it is believed, attract flying insects.

Stridulation The production of noise as a means of communication in arthropods.

Sucking stomach The structure in the cephalothorax of spiders that is used to suck up the predigested liquid contents of its prey.

Tarantula A name which, strictly speaking, should only be applied to members of the genus *Lycosa* of the family *Lycosidae*, but which these days tends to be used to describe the hairy mygalomorph spiders.

Tracheae The tubes through which gas exchange takes place in insects and also in some spiders. These branch out throughout the body and carry oxygen directly to where it is needed.

Trichobothria Hairlike structures on the outer surface of arachnids, which, it is believed, detect vibrations and air currents.

INDEX

Credits
Photographs by Ken & Rod Preston-Mafham,
Premaphotos Wildlife!